"This is a much-needed st accessible history and theology of adoration rooted in the spirit of the postconciliar liturgical reforms. Edward Foley's book is especially pertinent in the church today as the practice of adoration, benediction, and other eucharistic devotions captivates the imaginations of younger Catholics in particular. In response, Foley has issued a clarion call for the renewal of eucharistic devotion in a way that respects the primacy of the church's liturgy. Foley brings together a solid theological grounding for adoration with concrete pastoral principles to guide its practice. He also broadens our theological approach to adoration by drawing connections to ecology and Christian ethics. This book is a must read for ministers and anyone interested in the history, theology, and practice of adoration."

— Nathan P. Chase, PhD, Assistant Professor of Liturgical and Sacramental Theology, Aquinas Institute of Theology

"The United States Catholic bishops have committed themselves to a multi-year eucharistic revival, crowned by a National Eucharistic Congress 17–21 July 2024. Edward Foley's *Eucharistic Adoration after Vatican II* provides a magnificent background and accompaniment to this program, indeed for any process intended to deepen eucharistic spirituality for the future. Marked by impressive tracing of the complex historical trajectories of eucharistic practice and devotions; a welcome account of the theological principles emerging from this history in the context of the reformed post-Vatican II Order of Mass; a sketch of an 'accessibly lived' eucharistic spirituality; and an outline of key principles and guidelines for renewed eucharistic liturgy and devotions, this short volume is the best guide I can think of for this initiative. I pray that everyone involved—laity, bishops, priests, deacons, catechists, members of religious communities, seminarians, and novices—would make Foley's accessible monograph required reading. It has my highest recommendation as a stunning example of fine scholarship and pastoral zeal brought into fruitful dialogue."

— Fr. Jan Michael Joncas

Eucharistic Adoration after Vatican II

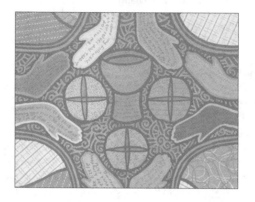

Edward Foley

LITURGICAL PRESS
Collegeville, Minnesota

www.litpress.org

1	2	3	4	5	6	7	8	9

Library of Congress Cataloging-in-Publication Data

Names: Foley, Edward, author.
Title: Eucharistic adoration after Vatican II / Edward Foley.
Description: Collegeville, Minnesota : Liturgical Press, [2022] | Includes
  bibliographical references. | Summary: "In Eucharistic Adoration after Vatican II,
  Edward Foley examines the relationship between Vatican II, liturgical prayer, and
  contemporary eucharistic adoration and devotions"—Provided by publisher.
Identifiers: LCCN 2022006364 (print) | LCCN 2022006365 (ebook) |
  ISBN 9780814644690 (paperback) | ISBN 9780814644928 (epub) |
  ISBN 9780814644928 (pdf)
Subjects: LCSH: Lord's Supper—Adoration. | Lord's Supper—Catholic Church. |
  Vatican Council (2nd : 1962–1965 : Basilica di San Pietro in Vaticano) | Catholic
  Church—Liturgy—History. | Catholic Church—Doctrines—History. | BISAC:
  RELIGION / Christian Rituals & Practice / Worship & Liturgy | RELIGION /
  Christianity / Catholic Classification: LCC BX2233 .F65 2022 (print) | LCC
  BX2233 (ebook) | DDC 264/.02036—dc23/eng/20220414
LC record available at https://lccn.loc.gov/2022006364
LC ebook record available at https://lccn.loc.gov/2022006365

Contents

Introduction

Having grown up in a very Catholic environment, eucharistic adoration and devotions were memorable and essential parts of my formative years. As a grade-schooler at St. Mary's of the Lake Parish in my hometown of Gary, Indiana, I learned to make visits to the Blessed Sacrament as a first grader. Even before I was allowed to receive first Communion, this involved practices of spiritual communion and even documenting my visits to the sacrament as part of "spiritual bouquets" that, with the help of my teachers, I crafted as gifts to parents and grandparents for various special occasions. A six-year-old does not have many resources for honoring such special folk in one's life. Being able to create a Mother's Day card filled with dozens of spiritual communions derived from visits to the Blessed Sacrament, therefore, was a mystical gift whose power and appreciative reception I remember vividly to this day.

When I became an altar server—we called them knights of the altar back then—serving Benediction of the Blessed Sacrament was a necessary practice for advancing through the ranks. Serving innumerable Masses and rites of Benediction was an essential stepping-stone for moving from apprentice to knight to knight commander to senior knight commander and, ultimately, to master knight. These ritual experiences were not only instrumental in progressing through what we then envisioned as the "altar boy chain of command"; they were also formative for my evolving vocation. I doubt that I would have entered a minor seminary in 1962 or eventually have been ordained a priest without them.

Eucharistic adoration, Benediction and its parallel devotions have been a part of my life and spirituality as long as I can remember. They have also been a bit of a paradox for me since I began studying liturgy and its history and theology. My high school seminary years were the years of the Second Vatican Council (1962–65). The ensuing years of studying philosophy and then theology unfolded in the wake of this breathtaking ecclesial event. During my theology studies in the early 1970s, each semester witnessed one more new ritual, one more new directive. The ritual explosion of those years was both chaotic and exhilarating.

In the many decades since those heady days, I have studied and analyzed, taught and promoted the liturgical reforms inaugurated by that historic council. For almost four decades, part of my teaching responsibilities included preparing seminarians to preside and preach at public worship. Thus, for decades I taught the official rites of the church reformed after Vatican II, including exposition and Benediction of the Blessed Sacrament. One of the quandaries that I have faced throughout the years is that what the reformed postconciliar eucharistic rites promote and allow is not always what people experience. There were radical changes in the eucharistic liturgy embedded in the Order of Mass promulgated by Pope St. Paul VI (d. 1978) in 1969. Beyond the use of the vernacular, these included a more dialogical format of the Mass, the transformation of the offertory rite to a preparation of gifts, a complete revision of the Lectionary, new eucharistic prayers, and Communion under both forms. At the same time, my multiple experiences of Benediction and other eucharistic devotions after the appearance of these innumerable reformed rites seem to be identical to what had been in place in the 1950s.

This book began in large part as a personal quest to address my own questions about the relationship of Vatican II and contemporary eucharistic adoration, Benediction, and devotions. Since my liturgical training was originally historical, chapter 1 is my instinctive attempt to provide a coherent overview of the very complex history of these practices. Beyond the historical contours of such devotions, it is important to discern what kind of theological principles have emerged from or are deeply embedded in our long tradition of eucharistic devotions. Chapter 2 is an effort to highlight these principles by employing the structure and texts of the reformed Order of Mass itself as the central prism for doing so. Because official theologies do not always have much of an impact on people's lives, the turn to spirituality is the focus of chapter 3. The driving question here concerns how authentic eucharistic practices impact day-to-day eucharistic living of the baptized. Each theological principle articulated in chapter 2 finds a parallel in chapter 3's vision for an accessibly lived eucharistic spirituality. Finally, since the actual enactments of eucharistic devotions and their allied practices are embodied acts of theology, in chapter 4 it seems essential to outline some key principles and guidelines to guide and safeguard the kinds of theologies and practical spiritualities that these practices nourish and encourage.

A foundational belief behind this writing is that devotions of every kind contribute in a unique and essential way to my personal faith and that of the wider church. This is especially true for eucharistic devotions, which touch what Vatican II called the fount and summit of the church's life (*Constitution on the Sacred Liturgy* 10).[1] My sincere hope is that this modest effort to renew my own eucharistic faith and practices might be of benefit to others as well.

Edward Foley, Capuchin
Solemnity of the Most Holy Body and Blood of Christ, 2021

Chapter One

Insights from History

Introduction

Theological investigations about a worship practice often begin with mapping out the origins and development of such a ritual. Sometimes the historical evidence is employed to justify some ongoing tradition or, contrarily, to refute any unwelcome innovation. The shorthand for these alternate approaches is the familiar "We've always done it that way" or its counterpart, "We've never done it that way." In this book, the historical arts are employed neither as some spiritual bludgeon nor as a religious roadblock for evolving religious practices and their theologies. Instead, these ancient testimonies provide a vital context for pondering the present. So we undertake this historical turn out of a deep belief that our histories provide wise lenses for navigating the present.

Three principles guide this current venture in attempting to provide some overview of the many historical strands that comprise the evolving story of eucharistic adoration and devotion. The first is the enduring insight that Christianity was born in pluriformity and only over a span of many centuries moved, with notable convulsions, to greater uniformity.[1] Symbolic of this aboriginal diversity was the need at the time of Jesus' death to display his name in three different languages on the cross

(John 19:20). This signaled in a striking way how multicultural-ity and divergence were hallmarks of emerging Christianity. Thus, there is a need to avoid homogenizing the rich traditions our creed calls catholic and compressing them into a single trajectory toward some presumed authentic practice.

A second principle concerns the appropriateness of trans-planting some documented practice from one historical epoch to another. Just because some idea or activity was an accepted or even a preferred teaching or practice in one era of Chris-tianity does not automatically justify relocating that same usage to another. It is well recognized that Roman Catholicism has experienced notable evolutions in authoritative teaching and acceptable ritualizing. Theologies and liturgical practices arise in specific historical and cultural contexts that do not always legitimate their continuation or replanting in some other different era and context. This is precisely why the church has reforms and reforming councils.

A third principle is grounded in the insights of James and Evelyn Whitehead.[2] These pioneers in the art of theological reflection were insistent that effective pastoral decision-making cannot be achieved by accessing only a single source of wisdom, such as canon law or papal teaching. Rather, their widely re-spected schema acknowledges three legitimate wisdom sources that must be engaged before pastoral decision-making occurs: religious tradition, the cultural context, and human experience. They also introduced a simple strategy that requires folk listen-ing to these various sources, then putting them into a respectful conversation, and only then moving toward some credible pastoral implementation.

In that spirit, this chapter is a venture in listening to our religious tradition and its teachings and practices of eucharistic adoration. This work alone will not allow us to suggest any pastoral decisions about this treasured practice. Rather, it will establish one of multiple resources that we will draw into a respectful theological dialogue, so that we might eventually provide some principles and guidelines for pastoral practice that are well anchored in our history.

Emerging Christianity and the Early Church

We have a very limited picture of early Christian ritualizing in all of its diversity. There are tantalizing hints that the sick were sometimes anointed by elders (Jas 5:14). We do not know, however, how widespread was this practice or exactly how people were anointed or prayed over in this ritual. Similarly, assorted writers noted that certain times of the day were appropriate for praying. Apart from many references to the Our Father, however, we do not know the content of such prayer. Even when there are passing references to "psalms," it is not clear that these are the Davidic psalms of the Old Testament. More startling, we do not even know the content, style, or length of eucharistic prayers employed at the center of the Lord's Supper. Writing in mid-second-century Rome, the revered apologist St. Justin Martyr (d. about 165) simply reports that the "president" offers the prayers and gives thanks "to the best of his ability," to which the assembly assents with an "Amen."[3]

The earliest centuries of emerging Christianity certainly provide indications of deep reverence for the Eucharist but none of what we now call adoration. St. Paul's tirade against the unethical eucharistic practices of the Corinthian community (1 Cor 11:17-22) forcefully drives this point home. Any disregard for others in celebrating the Lord's Supper is an affront to the living Body of Christ and a source of condemnation, as it shatters the unity of the community. For Paul, this *koinonia*—sometimes translated as "fellowship" or "communion"—was central.

What Paul and successive generations of writers make clear is that the great reverence and respect required of the Eucharist is first directed at the eucharistic action and the baptized who participate in that action. This is confirmed by Paul's subsequent chapter in his First Letter to the Corinthians, in which he praises the importance of a united community and asserts, "[Y]ou are the body of Christ" (1 Cor 12:27). The eucharistic elements were certainly honored by the emerging community. For example, Justin Martyr indicates in his writings that bread was sent to members who could not be physically present for the Lord's Supper. About the same time, St. Irenaeus of Lyon (flourished about 170) reported that eucharistic bread was also sent between churches as a symbol of unity and respect. This usage echoes the central concern of Paul about the unity of the body. At this stage, eucharistic elements even outside the celebration of the Lord's Supper served the distinctive purpose of strengthening the bonds of communion with absent members or distant churches.

These stories of eucharistic sharing are our first evidence that the elements were preserved outside of the Lord's Super, but ordinarily only until they could be shared. The baptized improvised means for transporting this sacred gift. Some images from the catacombs and descriptions found in early Christian writings suggest that baskets, small boxes, or even linen bags were employed for this purpose. It is possible that on some occasions the eucharistized bread was set aside in house churches or people's homes. St. Basil the Great (d. 379), for example, notes that it is appropriate for desert ascetics to have eucharistized bread in their hermitages so that they could self-communicate. He also acknowledges that throughout Egypt the laity ordinarily kept the Eucharist at home and participated in Communion when they desired.[4] Ancient equivalents of cupboards or closets as well as chests would have served the purpose of reserving the eucharistized bread. What we do not have in these centuries, however, is any evidence of adoration or other ritualizing around the reserved sacrament other than its being shared as Communion.

When evidence of adoration does appear, it is situated firmly within the eucharistic celebration itself. In his *Commentary on Psalm 98*, for example, St. Augustine (d. 430) instructs that "no one should eat this flesh unless he has first adored it."[5] Similarly, St. Cyril of Jerusalem (d. 386) offered a memorable baptismal instruction to the newly initiated on how to receive Communion with reverence, directing that we should make our left hand a "throne" for the right hand, since our right hand was about to receive the King.[6] In his commentary on the Gospel of Matthew, St. John Chrysostom (d. 407) urges his hearers to "follow the Magi" and similarly offer adoration when they come to the table.[7]

These witnesses also highlight liturgical texts as well as bodily acts of reverence incorporated into the liturgy for nourishing this devotion. In his commentary on the Gospel of Matthew, for example, Chrysostom cites a version of an ancient invitation to Communion still in use today: "holy things to the holy." This text is resonant with sources indicating that by the fourth century it became customary to show the bread and wine to the people during the eucharistic liturgy. More unusual is Cyril's description of the "hallowing" of the body by touching one's hands to their lips after drinking from the cup and touching one's eyes, forehead, and other senses. While such actions may strike contemporary readers as bizarre, they are in "continuity with a tradition that regarded the eucharist not only as spiritual food but also as a protective talisman against danger and illness."[8]

What will be new in the next era is the growing evidence of ritual reverence for Eucharist outside of the Mass: a development that seems to occur only in Western Christianity. As Robert Taft (d. 2018) notes:

> What is different about Eastern and Western Christian Eucharistic adoration is not its presence or absence, but

the fact that in the East it has remained where it was
throughout pre-Medieval Christendom East and West: in
the context of the Eucharistic liturgy and not as something
apart.[9]

The Early Medieval Period:
Sixth to Tenth Centuries

Introduction: Rome and many other great urban centers of
Christianity in the West were in steep decline in the fifth and
sixth centuries. It is estimated that at the height of the Roman
Empire, the population of the city of Rome may have been
800,000. By the time St. Gregory the Great (d. 604) became
Bishop of Rome, the population was well under 50,000 and
maybe even as low as 20,000. This urban decline as well as the
explosion of monasticism, especially under the influence of the
sixth-century Rule of Benedict (St. Benedict died in 547), shifted
the center of influence in the West from great bishops and their
dioceses to outstanding monks and their monasteries.

Germanization: Another important consideration for contex-
tualizing this era is the growing impact of the "Germanic"
tribes and the spiritual sensitivities that they spread across
Europe. James Russell has argued that the many tribes grouped
under this Germanic umbrella brought with them a religious
imagination that was different from that of early Christians.
Russell broadly characterizes this religious imagination as
more magical, distinguishing it from the more ethical and doctrinal viewpoints that marked emerging Christianity. This
different spiritual worldview and consciousness would have
a significant impact on many aspects of Christianity, including
worship. Particularly important is the Germanic tendency to
display a distinctive valuing of sacred spaces, to create notable
physical distance between ordinary folk and their priests,
and to exhibit an increased focus on the objects employed in
worship.[10]

While these new spiritual instincts are not completely foreign to those held by many in previous eras, Germanized Christians developed them in sometimes dramatic fashion. For example, already in earlier centuries, great emphasis had been placed on certain devotional places. The "nun" Egeria, who is thought to have penned an account of her pilgrimage to the Holy Land at the end of the fourth century, is probably the most celebrated witness to this spiritual impulse in the early church. Her travelogue documents treasured shrines in the Holy Land that attracted flocks of pilgrims. With the monasticization of the early medieval church, however, this instinct for pilgrimage became both domesticated and miniaturized. To provide a substitute for travel to the Holy Sepulcher in Jerusalem or to the tomb of St. Peter in Rome, symbolic replicas of these places—including chapels or altars bearing their names—were constructed within the walls of monasteries. Therefore, instead of undertaking a long and sometimes dangerous trip to a holy destination, monks often took daily expeditions to symbolic substitutes inside their enclosure, where a relic of the true cross replaced Golgotha or a thread from the Blessed Virgin's veil became Bethlehem.

Altars: The later centuries of the early church provide evidence that altars were a focus of devotion and even healing. One famous example was narrated by St. Gregory of Nazianzus (d. 390). In his funeral oration for his sister, Gorgonia, this Doctor of the Church describes that when she was dangerously ill, Gorgonia visited the altar in a favorite church building. Gregory relates that during this private visit, which occurred in the middle of the night, Gorgonia approached the altar and even rested her head on it in prayer to Jesus, the Divine Physician.[11] The honoring of altars was greatly amplified during this period. It was common, for example, for monks to make private visits to the main altar in the monastery. This was not visiting the Blessed Sacrament, which in this period was not reserved on the altar. Rather, the altar was reverenced for its central role in the eucharistic action and considered an important symbol of Christ. This understanding is reflected in contemporary traditions of kissing, dressing, incensing, and bowing to the altar. The 1978 ritual for the *Dedication of a Church and an Altar* reiterates the ancient teaching, confirming that "[t]he altar is Christ" (4:4). Notable in this early medieval period was not only reverence for the altar but also the growing multiplication of altars within the same building. A striking symbol of this tendency is a celebrated floor plan of the monastery grounds at St. Gall in present-day Switzerland, which included an astonishing 17 altars in the church and various chapels in the monastery. This idealized plan from the early ninth century well characterizes the growing significance of altars within a monastic compound during the medieval period of our history.

Relics: Related to altar devotion was the growing importance of relics, especially those of the martyrs. Their significance would eventually eclipse that of altars and become one of the most powerful devotional forces in the medieval church. Christians of the first centuries venerated the burial places of martyrs, such as the catacombs or tombs. The tomb of the martyred bishop St. Polycarp (d. 155) was already venerated by his followers in Smyrna around 160 or so. What these early centuries did not witness, however, was the excavation, division, and dissemination of these remains. Charles Freeman suggests that in Rome, for example, church leaders were afraid that if they distributed any relics of the apostles or martyrs buried in their confines, doing so could lessen the sacred power of the city itself and, therefore, of its bishop.[12]

One of the most important relics discovered in the fourth century was the true cross, which, tradition reports, was uncovered by St. Helena, the mother of the emperor Constantine, around 328. The excavations sponsored by Helena uncovered three crosses thought to be those of Jesus and the two criminals executed with him (Matt 27:38). Since it was not clear which was the Lord's cross, each in turn was touched to a woman who had long suffered some unnamed disease. The miraculous cure of the woman touched by the wood of one of the crosses verified which was the "true" cross. This story underscores a key power of all "true" relics: they are believed to have miraculous power. Helena took the cross along with the uncovered holy nails, thought to be employed in Jesus' crucifixion, back to Constantinople. At the same time, she left some part of the true cross carefully preserved in silver for the bishop of Jerusalem.[13] The previously mentioned Egeria reports that this relic was brought out for veneration by the faithful on the morning of Good Friday. It was held firmly in the hands of the bishop with deacons guarding at his side while the faithful came up to kiss the sacred wood. Such watchfulness was necessary because someone previously engaged in this ritual apparently bit off a piece of this invaluable relic and ran off with it.[14] This curious event foreshadows a common problem throughout the middle ages that attests to the immeasurable value of these treasures: relic theft.[15]

According to Freeman, St. Ambrose of Milan (d. 397) was a pivotal figure in rethinking the power of relics. Rather than believing that dispersing relics would diminish his authority, as some bishops of Rome had held, Ambrose believed that relics could be an avenue for exercising personal power if he dispatched them to colleagues and admirers. Notable in this era was the multiplication of holy sites that, unlike Jerusalem or Rome, were largely unconnected with the events of Jesus' life or the legendary activities of his first followers.[16] It is difficult to overestimate not only the spiritual but also the economic and political impact of these sites and their relics on medieval Europe. Pilgrims flocked to such shrines seeking their miraculous powers. Accommodating the multiple needs of pilgrims—housing, food, and even religious souvenirs—spawned enormous secondary economies around these holy sites that in turn, boosted the prestige not only of the place but also of local civic and ecclesiastical leaders. More than spiritual attractions or economic engines, Freeman concludes, these shrines were important places of social refuge and safe havens in a violent and disintegrating world.[17]

Geary demonstrates that for multiple reasons, relics became the primary focus of religious devotion throughout Europe beginning in the eighth century. That relics eclipsed the altar as a devotional focus is illustrated by the growing requirement that any altar employed for eucharistic celebration must contain a relic of a martyr, a tradition affirmed by the Second Council of Nicaea in 787 (canon 7). It was not until the 1978 rite for the *Dedication of a Church and an Altar* that this requirement was changed and relics were no longer allowed to be placed within an altar but only beneath it. More dramatically, relics were no longer required for dedicating an altar (4:5).

Commodification and Objectification: Relics slowly evolved from vehicles important for mediating the power and virtue of a holy individual to their treatment as "sacred prestige commodities."[18] This process—broadly documented in the way relics were stolen, traded, counterfeited, and wielded as symbols of power through the medieval period—has much resonance with the characteristics of Germanization noted earlier. Increasingly relics were less about prodding believers to ethical living and more valued and authenticated by their miraculous powers. These instincts of commodification, unmoored from any ethical or spiritual framework, remain with us even today.

The relics of martyrs who imitated Christ by giving up their lives have been especially prized throughout history. The rite for the *Dedication of a Church and an Altar* notes that, while all saints can be considered witnesses of Christ, "the witness of blood has a special significance, which is given complete and perfect expression by depositing only martyrs' relics beneath the altar" (4:5). It is not surprising, therefore, that perception about the eucharistic bread could evolve into treating it as a prized sacramental relic of the aboriginal Christian martyr:

Jesus Christ. Evidence of this belief is confirmed by the documented practice of depositing parts of consecrated hosts in an
altar as part of its consecration. This is reported in a document
outlining the dedication of churches from the early eighth
century (*Roman Ordinal* 42:11). From around the same period
there are reports that Christians such as St. Birinus (d. 650),
the first bishop of Dorchester, were buried with consecrated
hosts or even small containers of consecrated wine. Such practices signal the evolving trend to separate the use of consecrated elements from the eucharistic liturgy or its traditional
extension through Communion to the sick or to others in need.
Theological developments in the next period will greatly in-
tensify this trend.

The Late Medieval Period:
Eleventh to Fifteenth Centuries

The developments around eucharistic devotion in the late
medieval period are well understood as organic developments
from the previous period. The Germanizing tendencies high-
lighting the sacrality of vessels such as patens and chalices,
the growing importance of relics, and the treatment of the
consecrated elements as the ultimate relics continued, as did
the ritualization around Eucharist apart from the celebration
of the Mass. However, the explosion of eucharistic devotions
that characterize this era required some catalysts to trigger this
dramatic expansion. One key impetus was emerging eucharistic controversies.

Eucharistic Controversies: The late ninth century witnessed
the first systematic speculations about the nature of eucharistic
presence in the Christian West. Earlier theologians had confirmed the ancient belief that Christ was truly present in the
eucharistic species, but none had attempted to explain in any
detail the nature of that presence. This changed when the monk

Paschasius (d. about 860) composed a treatise he entitled *On the Body and Blood of the Lord*. Written to instruct the monks of his Benedictine abbey at Corbie in modern-day France, Paschasius developed an original theology of presence by equating the sacramental body of Christ with the body of the historical Jesus. He concluded that what we receive in Communion is identical to the body born of Mary. This innovative yet problematic thinking signaled a major shift in the eucharistic equation that reverberates yet today.

Pope St. John Paul II (d. 2005) was a great fan of the theologian Henri de Lubac, whom he created a cardinal in 1983. De Lubac's famed study of the "body of Christ" demonstrated that over the centuries Christianity has recognized three modes of Christ's real presence: the historical body of Jesus, the ecclesial body of his followers, and the consecrated elements or sacramental body.[19] De Lubac gives special attention to the concept of the "mystical Body" (*corpus mysticum*). Contemporary usage, such as in the 1943 encyclical *Mystici Corporis* (The Mystical Body) of Pope Pius XII (d. 1958), asserts that the mystical Body is the church. De Lubac's exhaustive study, however, demonstrates that from its first appearance in the fifth century, the term did not refer to the church but to the consecrated host. The church, on the other hand, was the *corpus verum* or "true body," of Christ.

The original connection between the historical and ecclesial bodies of Christ—confirmed by St. Paul (1 Cor 12:27) and reiterated by theologians such as St. Augustine[20]—was challenged by these new theologies. Instead of the foundational pairing of the ecclesial and historical bodies, there emerged a new pairing between the historical Jesus with the consecrated host. Eventually the equation *baptized = historical body = true Body of Christ* was eclipsed by the new configuration *consecrated host = historical body = true Body of Christ*. The power of this new equation will have many enduring effects; two are of particular note for this study. First is the heightened importance of the eucharistic elements—especially the bread—apart from the eucharistic action and the ecclesial body's diminished role in that action. A second is the theological diminishment of the baptized: no longer considered the "true" but now the "mystical" body of Christ.

Gary Macy has aptly described eucharistic theology and especially the topic of eucharistic real presence as the "nuclear physics" of the medieval period. For centuries theologians debated the nature of this presence.[21] While these disputes raged in university settings and the highest echelons of the church, popular devotions were taking their own course.

Seeing the Host: One growing need among the faithful was what Edouard Dumoutet famously called *Le désir de voir l'Hostie,* or "the desire to see the host." The reasons for this craving were multiple. One significant factor was an evolving self-awareness of the laity, who no longer viewed themselves as the Body of Christ and instead assumed a more diminished self-awareness as a community of penitents. Particular developments such as the theology of original sin and the prominent threat of purgatory after death loomed large in this development. Already in the fifth century, some bishops voiced concern about declining numbers of the baptized receiving Communion. That number declined so dramatically in the ensuing centuries that the Fourth Lateran Council in 1215 had to mandate that people go to Communion at least once a year.

A pervasive sense of unworthiness among the baptized and the looming threat of purgatory or even damnation dissuaded many faithful from physical Communion. Some theologians even argued that unworthy reception of blessed bread—a common substitute for Eucharist—also resulted in mortal sin. Increasingly perceived as a potentially dangerous act, reception of Communion held the possibility of becoming not only an unworthy event but even a sacrilegious one. This was true even for the clergy who presided at Eucharist, as evidenced by the many personal prayers of contrition and unworthiness that became embedded in the texts of the medieval Mass.

A safer practice, resonant with devotions for venerating relics, was watching the host. Initially this occurred within the Mass itself with the introduction of the elevation of the bread after its consecration. According to Gary Macy, there was already some evidence in the twelfth century of raising the host during the words of consecration.[22] However, new theological controversies triggered the practice of elevating the consecrated bread immediately *after* the words of consecration. Some theologians held that the bread was not consecrated until after the cup was consecrated as well. To counter this position and to demonstrate that the bread was fully consecrated before the cup, the practice of elevating the newly consecrated bread was introduced in Paris in the twelfth century. This innovation, signaled by the ringing of bells and even illumination with a special candle, prompted a new prayer practice on the part of the laity: saluting the host with short prayers. Nathan Mitchell suggests that this practice originated with the priest "saluting" the host before receiving Communion. The introduction of the elevation not only transferred this practice to a different moment in the liturgy but expanded it from clergy to laity.[23]

This new form of adoration within the eucharistic liturgy is in continuity with previous practices such as acts of reverence immediately before Communion. What is new, however, is the singular and sustained emphasis on the host alone rather than in conjunction with the consecrated cup. Eventually, a miraculous power was ascribed to this act of watching the elevated host, or "ocular Communion." It was widely believed, for example, that gazing at the raised host promised a safe delivery for a pregnant mother, paused the suffering of beloved dead in purgatory, ensured safe arrival for traveler, and forestalled the aging process. Gazing at the elevated host became the ritual center of the Mass for the laity. There is testimony that the baptized would often move from one side altar to another or even from church to church to witness the elevation. This intraliturgical act of adoration became a critical springboard for the growing and varied practices of eucharistic adoration outside of the celebration of Mass. As Gary Macy concludes,

> This extensive devotion to the sacrament represented a completely new attitude toward the Eucharist. Before the twelfth century no similar devotion to the real presence appears in the history of Western Christianity. Yet by the middle of the thirteenth century, most of the liturgical, devotional, and even superstitious forms which this attitude would take had been established.[24]

The Reserved Sacrament, Easter Sepulchers, and Monstrances: A parallel development during this period was growing acts of devotion to the reserved sacrament. It was ordinary for acolytes to carry candles before the gospel book and other sacred objects. That practice eventually transferred over to the consecrated bread. Among other things, the tenth-century monastic directive known as the *Regularis Concordia* (Monastic Agreement) instructs how to bring Communion to a sick brother directly from the altar at the conclusion of Mass: this includes a procession led by acolytes and a thurifer.[25] Slowly, there developed the related practice of keeping a burning light next to the reserved sacrament. Because of security concerns around the consecrated species, legislation eventually dictated that the elements should be kept under lock and key (Fourth Lateran Council, 20). Usually, this meant a wall tabernacle or a "tabernacle house" within the church. Eventually tabernacles migrated to the main altar, which became the ordinary location for the reserved sacrament and a sanctuary lamp.

Macy contends that the twelfth century provides our first witnesses to prayer before the reserved species.[26] St. Thomas Becket (d. 1170) told King Henry II (d. 1189) that he prayed for him "before the Majesty of the Body of Christ."[27] In the ensuing centuries there would be multiple stories of saints and blesseds who would spend hours in prayer before the reserved species, especially during the Triduum.

A unique eucharistic vessel that developed during this period was the Easter sepulcher, which grew out of a dramatic practice reported in *Regularis Concordia*.[28] That highly influential document contains rubrics and texts for a very early form of what we would today call liturgical drama. On Holy Saturday, monks buried the cross and then kept watch at this symbolic tomb throughout the night. Before Easter Matins the sacristan removed the cross, and during Easter Matins the monks briefly reenacted the Easter morning encounter between the women and the angel recorded in the gospels (e.g., Matt 28:1-7). From the same era, a *Life of Saint Ulrich* reports a similar practice, but instead of a cross being buried, a consecrated host was symbolically entombed.[29] Easter sepulchers would continue to be constructed and used well into the sixteenth century, especially in England.

No liturgical vessel is more symbolic of eucharistic developments in the late Middle Ages than the monstrance. Its origin was quite practical. If seeing the host had become the ritual center of the Mass, it was natural to create a vehicle for extending this highlight beyond the confines of the liturgy and the capacity of the priest, who was sometimes urged (and even paid) to hold the host up higher and longer. Some monstrances were modeled after reliquaries of the time, which held relics in a glass cylinder. This evolution was an implicit acknowledgment that the host was understood to be the ultimate Christian relic and, by consequence, Christ was honored as the supreme martyr. Sometimes a simple holder for exposing the consecrated host was built into a tabernacle. Eventually, the monstrance developed into a distinctive vessel consisting of a stem with a node and a flat window for holding a large consecrated host. The first clear literary evidence of such vessels comes from the life of St. Dorothea of Montau (d. 1394). Her biographer reported about Dorothea's intense devotion to the Blessed

Sacrament and described how the Eucharist was daily displayed for her in a primitive monstrance. This occurred when she was living the life of an anchoress or religious hermit in a cell inside a church.[30] As monstrances evolved, they were sometimes designed to blend with the surrounding architecture. In ensuing centuries, they would become permanent elements in many sanctuaries, often centered in a soaring reredos, or elaborate wall decoration at the back of the high altar.

During this period, eucharistic worship outside of Mass was established as a staple of lay piety. In 1452, the Council of Cologne already provided instructions for the exposition of the Blessed Sacrament.[31] Eamon Duffy summarizes this evolution by noting that by this point "for most of the people, most of the time the Host was something to be seen, not to be consumed."[32] In many ways, adoration of the Blessed Sacrament became the pinnacle of Christian ritual life. Symbolic of this liturgical dominance was the permission given by Pope Leo X (d. 1521) for Mass in the presence of the Blessed Sacrament (*Missa in coram Sanctissimo Sacramentum*). This custom already appeared in 1372,[33] and it was widely understood as a way to add more solemnity to the eucharistic celebration.

There was some pushback to this growing practice. Cardinal Nicholas of Cusa (d. 1464), the one-time vicar general for the Papal States, famously noted that the Blessed Sacrament had been instituted as food and not for display. More broadly, various entities in Rome expressed concern that exposition was being employed to provide an extra solemnization of a feast or even a funeral. In response, the Sacred Congregation of Rites forbade the celebration of Mass on an altar where the Blessed Sacrament was exposed. It also disallowed exposition during the last three days of Holy Week and generally counseled against too-frequent exposition.[34] The 1917 *Code of Canon Law* repeated some of the same restrictions to the practice, already articulated in the 1452 Council of Cologne over which Cardinal de Cusa presided. It is notable that outside the octave of *Corpus Christi* (the Body of Christ), public exposition of the Blessed Sacrament was not allowed except for grave reason and with permission of the bishop (canon 1274).

Medieval Women, Spiritual Communion, and the Feast of Corpus Christi: One distinctive population drawn to eucharistic adoration in this period was women mystics. This is documented by the *Ancrene Wisse*[35] (also known as *Ancrene Riwle*), a manual for women hermits. It was written between 1225 and 1240 for three sisters, each of whom chose to be walled up inside a cell adjacent to a church in the same manner as the previously mentioned anchoress St. Dorothea.

Each of these cells was to have three windows, one of which allowed the women to observe Mass and take Communion. The *Ancrene Wisse* prescribed that as the anchoress began the daily course of prayer, she was to sprinkle herself with holy water and direct her eyes through one window to ponder the "flesh of God and his precious blood" above the high altar. This is a reference to the reserved sacrament suspended in a pyx. She was then to offer a series of salutations to the reserved sacrament (e.g., "Hail, provision on our pilgrimage"), followed by a short prayer. This and other texts were repeated at the elevation of the host during Mass.[36]

Another important group of medieval women who had great devotion to the Eucharist were Beguines.[37] The Beguines were a religious movement of women who lived a form of lay religious life in the world. Sometimes gathered into communities, sometimes living alone, they supported themselves with work such as lace making while they served those in need and devoted themselves to prayer and contemplation. Originating around Liège at the end of the twelfth century, this new form of apostolic life in Belgium and elsewhere received approval in the early thirteenth century from the recently elected Pope Honorius III (d. 1227) at the request of Canon Jacques de Vitry of Liège. De Vitry's writings highlight the deep eucharistic devotion of several Beguines who desired frequent Communion and showed deep devotion to the reserved sacrament. He described how one Beguine, Marie of Oignies (d. 1213), was so dedicated to the Eucharist that after Mass she would remain for an extended period contemplating the empty chalice that remained on the altar.[38]

Another notable Beguine was the mystic Mechthild of Magdeburg (d. about 1282). Her extensive writings attest to both a deep eucharistic devotion and to the importance of mystical or spiritual communion. According to the *Ancrene Wisse*, an anchoress was allowed Communion only fifteen times a year. Beguines received much more often—sometimes weekly or even daily—for which they "practically waged war against their confessors and superiors to attain permission."[39] Mechthild pens a particular complaint "that she hears no Mass nor Hours and [yet] How God Praises her in ten things."

> I who am Divine am truly in you.
> I can never be sundered from you:
> However far we be parted,
> never can we be separated.
> I am in you and you are in Me.
> We could not be any closer.
> We two are fused into one,
> poured into a single mould.
> Thus, unwearied,
> we shall remain
> forever.[40]

This intense expression of mystical communion epitomizes a trend in which spiritual communion was theologically affirmed and pastorally promoted. Gary Macy describes how theologians of the era increasingly distinguished between receiving the physical sacrament and receiving its spiritual benefits. Prominent was the medieval theologian Hugh of St. Victor (d. 1141), who emphasized spiritual union with Christ as a union that was "far more important than, and can . . . exist apart from, either the outward ritual or the real presence."[41]

Some theologians and clergy were concerned that frequent Communion could breed indifference to the sacrament. Preachers of the period often emphasized that spiritual communion brought all of the benefits but incurred none of the risks of actual Communion. Dutch theologian Wessel Gansfort (d. 1489), for example, "went so far to argue that spiritual communion was superior to sacramental Communion because it was not restricted to specific times, places or persons." Eventually printed guides to Mass in this period included prayers for spiritual communion to be recited by the laity during the priest's Communion at Mass.[42]

St. Juliana of Liège (d. 1258) came under the influence of the followers of Marie of Oignies. In 1210, she received a recurring vision that featured a full moon with a darkened segment. Over time, Juliana interpreted the darkened segment as a feast that was missing from the church year. Eventually, Juliana accepted as her vocation the task of initiating and promoting this new feast.[43] Because of the many influential clerics around Liège, this feast was ultimately approved and promoted. Pope Urban IV (d. 1264)—the one-time archdeacon of Liège—established the feast for the universal church. Popes Martin V (d. 1431) and Eugene IV (d. 1447) granted special indulgences to those who participated in *Corpus Christi* processions. With its elaborate processions and surrounding pageantry, *Corpus Christi* is an apt summary of burgeoning eucharistic devotions in the late medieval period. The respected historian Miri Rubin goes even further suggesting that the cult solemnized by this feast was the central symbol of Christian culture at the end of the Middle Ages and the procession with the host was the epitome of the sacramental system.[44] The looming challenges of the sixteenth-century Protestant reforms would splinter that cultural system and its sacramental center in many places. In an early response to these challenges, the 1551 decree *Concerning the Most Holy Sacrament of the Eucharist* from the Council of Trent (1545–63) defended both the practice of adoration as well as the feast of *Corpus Christi* (chap. 5).

The Sixteenth to the Twentieth Centuries

The sixteenth century was a time of serious upheaval in Western Christianity. The Protestant Reformation in Europe ignited a splintering of Christianity that continues into the present day. While Protestant reformers could agree on key issues such as the primacy of Scripture, worship was an altogether different arena. In a famous gathering of ten leaders of the reform at Marburg Castle in 1529—including Martin Luther (d. 1546) and Ulrich Zwingli (d. 1531)—the issue of eucharistic presence was a central point of disagreement, which contributed greatly to the emergence of multiple Christian denominations.

The Protestant Reformation and its new eucharistic traditions had a dramatic impact on adoration in large segments of Christianity. In the more radical reforms, such as those enacted by Zwingli in Zurich, elaborate high altars and tabernacles were removed and related practices of eucharistic reservation and adoration were eliminated. Luther took a more moderate approach. While his writings demonstrate that he was against reserving the sacrament, he yet continued practices of adoration within the Lord's Supper itself, including an elevation of the consecrated elements in the ritual. He also allowed Communion to be brought to the sick in their homes; a practice that exists in some Lutheran congregations to this day[45] and continues within some Methodist and Presbyterian communities as well. Maybe surprising to many Roman Catholics, some Lutheran congregations today practice eucharistic reservation against Luther's instruction. Maxwell Johnson asks, "Can there be a place in Lutheranism for a eucharistic reservation that does not compromise the Lutheran Confessional focus on sacramental *usus* [use] or *actio* [action]?" He answers in the affirmative, noting that some Lutheran congregations "have obviously concluded that eucharistic reservation is an appropriate Lutheran option today."[46] Eucharistic reservation is even more widespread among Anglicans and Episcopalians, even though it was expressly forbidden in the 1662 *Book of Common Prayer.* Some contemporary Anglo-Catholic communities even practice Benediction, and the 1991 *Anglican Service Book* contains a rite for "Benediction of the Blessed Sacrament."

While eucharistic reservation and adoration outside of the Lord's Supper were rejected by most groups of reforming Protestants, eucharistic adoration expanded throughout Roman Catholicism in this period. This included the burgeoning practice of Forty Hours Devotion, as well as the growth of religious communities dedicated to perpetual adoration. Among the laity, visits to the Blessed Sacrament became a well-accepted pious devotion.

Forty Hours Devotion: The number forty is significant throughout biblical literature. During the great flood, rain fell on the earth for forty days and nights (Gen 7:11); Moses spent a similar amount of time on Mount Sinai (Exod 24:18); the Israelites wandered for forty years in the desert (Num 32:13); the prophet Elijah fasted on his forty-day journey to Mount Horeb; and Jesus fasted for forty days before the start of his public ministry. Thus, it is not surprising that a tradition calculates that Jesus spent forty hours in the tomb before his resurrection, an interpretation already reported by St. Augustine.[47]

It is this symbolic imaging that in large part helped fuel the development of Forty Hours Devotion. Since the second century, there has existed a forty-hour fast among Jesus' followers before the annual celebration of Easter. Josef Jungmann documents traditions of fasting, penance, and the uninterrupted reading of the Psalms to honor the hours Jesus spent in the tomb. This honoring eventually gravitated toward a temporary sepulcher in which a cross or even the consecrated bread was symbolically buried while monks kept watch. At the same time, gradual efforts to move the Easter vigil ever earlier on Holy Saturday—even into the morning—eventually diminished the possibility of any true forty-hour vigil.[48]

A more immediate trigger to this devotional development was the social and political tumult of the early sixteenth century. 1527 was a pivotal date here. This was the tenth anniversary of Luther's posting of his ninety-five theses. Furthermore, it was also a year of much political upheaval in Europe including the sack of Rome by Charles the V (d. 1558), the war over the Duchy of Milan, and critical military battles with the expanding threat of the Ottoman Empire on Christianity's eastern border. During a series of Lenten sermons that year, Fr. Antonio Belotti (d. 1528) urged members of the confraternity he founded at the Church of the Holy Sepulcher in Milan to pray for forty hours before the Blessed Sacrament four times a year.[49] This practice extended to other Milanese churches after his death with the help of the newly established Barnabite community, who apparently inaugurated the rotation of this devotion between churches. Philip Neri (d. 1595) introduced this devotion to Rome, and the Jesuits were also important advocates. Capuchin Giuseppe Piantanida of Ferno (d. 1556) was a tireless promoter of this practice. His Capuchin brothers helped spread the practice across Italy. It spread throughout Europe and even to the Americas when Bishop John Neumann (d. 1860) introduced the practice in Philadelphia and the Second Council of Baltimore (1866) officially introduced it throughout the United States.[50]

Pope Paul III (d. 1549) approved the practice of Forty Hours Devotion in 1539, as did Pius IV (d. 1565) in 1560. More important was the 1592 instruction of Clement VIII that established the uninterrupted practice of Forty Hours Devotions across the churches of Rome. The instruction characterized this devotion as publicly praying "before the face of the Lord."[51] More recently, Pope St. John Paul II affirmed the practice in his 1980 letter *Dominicae Cenae* (On the Mystery and Worship of the Eucharist 3). St. Charles Borromeo (d. 1584), archbishop of Milan, provided rather extensive rubrics for the celebration of Forty Hours Devotions in the "Ambrosian Sacramentary" for the Archdiocese of Milan.[52] So did Pope Clement XI in 1705, thus largely regulating the prayer until Vatican II. An adaptation of this Clementine Instruction was published in the *Roman Ritual* of 1952. Since the reforms of Vatican II, there is no official Roman ritual for Forty Hours Devotion. The 1973 ritual for Holy Communion and Worship of the Eucharist outside Mass does not speak of any Forty Hours Devotion but only addresses the practice of "lengthy exposition" (86–88).

Perpetual Adoration and Religious Communities: The practice of perpetual adoration was foreshowed by the Milanese and Roman tradition of rotating Forty Hours Devotions between churches in those cities. It was not a huge leap from a city-wide form of perpetual adoration to that located in a single church or chapel. One caveat is that perpetual adoration was not originally or always synonymous with exposition of the Blessed Sacrament.

The first evidence of perpetual adoration relates to the 1226 victory of King Louis VIII (d. 1226) over the heretical Albigensians. After Louis took control of Avignon, an Albigensian stronghold, he requested that the Blessed Sacrament be placed (not exposed) on the altar of a chapel in the Church of the Holy Cross in the city. This was both an act of thanksgiving and a ritual rebuke of the Albigensians, who denied that the Eucharist was the body of Christ. The huge numbers who participated in the adoration prompted the local bishop to allow this veiled exposition to continue indefinitely. This practice was eventually approved under Honorius III (d. 1216).[53] In the fourteenth century, there emerged a religious community apparently dedicated to eucharistic adoration: *Religiosi bianchi del corpo del Gesù Christo* (White Religious of the Body of Jesus Christ).

Clearer evidence of perpetual adoration is a sixteenth-century phenomenon, paralleling the rise of Forty Hours Devotion. At the end of the sixteenth century, King Philip II of Spain (d. 1598) established a eucharistic practice at the monastery of San Lorenzo in the royal residence of San Lorenzo de El Escorial, designed with successive pairs of religious praying night and day before the Blessed Sacrament.[54] This practice was slowly institutionalized, particularly in seventeenth-century France. Some of these ventures were diocesan. The earliest example is Chartres in 1658, in which all the churches were opened from 6:00 a.m. to 6:00 p.m. for adoration. That diocese further directed that each religious community with a chapel was to continue adoration night and day.[55] Similar efforts spread to other French dioceses up until the French Revolution (1789). There were also particular churches such as Saint-Sulpice in Paris that established perpetual adoration in 1648 as an act of reparation for a previous act of sacrilege against the reserved sacrament. These local practices were often supported by lay associations dedicated to perpetual adoration. These were the successors of local organizations dedicated to the Blessed Sacrament, like those established as the feast of *Corpus Christi* emerged.[56] In the nineteenth century, multiple adoration societies appeared. Some were dedicated to adoration at night, such as the French Nocturnal Adoration Society founded in 1848; others, such as the Belgian Archconfraternity of Perpetual Adoration, promoted perpetual adoration.

Multiple religious communities dedicated to the Eucharist and even to perpetual adoration emerged as well. Central to the foundation of the Clerics Regular Minor or Adorno Fathers in 1588 was a commitment to perpetual adoration. This was also true of the Congregation of the Sacred Heart of Jesus and Mary (Society of Picpus) established in 1594. Founded in 1636, the Congregation of the Blessed Sacrament, or the Dominicans of Perpetual Adoration, evolved from the Dominican Order. Better known is the Congregation of the Blessed Sacrament, founded by Peter Julian Eymard (d. 1868) and committed to fostering devotion to the Eucharist. A number of women's communities dedicated to perpetual adoration also emerged, including the Religious of the Perpetual Adoration (originally founded in 1526 but turning to perpetual adoration in 1789) and the Franciscan Sisters of Perpetual Adoration (founded 1849 and initiating perpetual adoration in 1878). The late eighteenth century also witnessed the establishment of a Priests' League for Adoration. Some of these communities, like the Franciscan Sisters of Perpetual Adoration, have reshaped their adoration practices, which are now reduced to daily adoration from 6:00 a.m. to 10:00 p.m. They yet retain perpetual adoration in their name, signaling their commitment to continue adoration to the extent possible with declining numbers.

One place that had a notable impact on eucharistic adoration and its theology was led by Mere Angélique Arnauld (d. 1661). At an early age she became the abbess of the Cistercian monastery of Port-Royal, which she later transferred from outside Versailles to Paris. Under her reform, Port-Royal became an important spiritual center aligned with the theologians of the movement known as Jansenism, emphasizing people's depravity and corruption. This created problems around sacraments, especially eucharistic reception. Since humans were perceived to be so utterly unworthy, Angélique promoted voluntary abstinence from Communion, claiming that such could be a mark of holiness equal to that of actual reception.[57] Part of cultivating this "sacrament of desire" as a prized reimagining of spiritual communion was the promotion of adoration as the primary task of Christians, trumping all others.[58] Angélique's sister Agnes refined this belief by suggesting that lay Christians offer Eucharist chiefly by adoring the sacrament while the ordained offer Eucharist by confecting it.[59] Angélique promoted all-night adoration, eventually leaving the Cistercians and establishing a new Institute of the Blessed Sacrament. While much of Jansenism was officially condemned, its influence lingered, especially the medieval belief about the danger of receiving Communion and the safer practice of adoration and spiritual communion.

Benediction, Holy Hours, and Visits to the Blessed Sacrament:
Benediction did not originate in this period, but it was during
this era that it developed as a distinctive ritual not linked to
other ceremonies. Its twofold roots were a popular form of
evening prayer and the rituals of *Corpus Christi*.[60] As for the
former, it was common in the thirteenth century to celebrate
evening devotions known as *laude* (praises) honoring the
Blessed Virgin. To lend special solemnity to this devotion, it
became widely accepted in the next century to celebrate *laude*
in the presence of the exposed sacrament. A second source
seems to have been the practice of stopping at designated
places during a *Corpus Christi* procession and blessing the
faithful with the sacrament. This practice was resonant with
the more ancient ritual of blessing folk with relics of saints or
even the true cross.

The earliest evidence of blessing folk with the Blessed Sacrament comes from a 1301 *Corpus Christi* procession in Hilde-
sheim, Germany. Before processing to the main altar, a monk
stopped in the middle of the choir, ascended the steps of the
altar, and blessed the assembly with a pyx containing the Sacrament.[61] This increasingly popular practice was always part
of a larger ritual. Benediction, very similar to present-day practice, is outlined in the 1614 *Roman Ritual* as the closing segment
of the *Corpus Christi* procession, while much simpler blessings
with the sacrament are appended to the Rite for Communion
to the Infirm.[62] As Mitchell rightly notes, it was not until 1958
that a decree of the Sacred Congregation of Rites affirmed
Benediction as a "true liturgical function."[63]

In the seventeenth century, devotion to the Sacred Heart of
Jesus became intimately connected with eucharistic adoration
and Benediction. As a child, St. Margaret Mary Alacoque
(d. 1690) was deeply devoted to the Blessed Sacrament. After
becoming a Visitation nun, she experienced visions while praying before the Blessed Sacrament and around the feast of *Corpus
Christi*. Jesus revealed to her his Sacred Heart and directed her

to receive Communion as often as allowed, especially on the first Friday of each month. She was also instructed to prostrate in prayer every Thursday between 11:00 p.m. and midnight, echoing the gospel reproach to the disciples in Gethsemane, "[C]ould you not stay awake with me one hour?" (Matt 26:40). The Lord also wished that a feast honoring his heart be established the Friday after the Octave of *Corpus Christi* in reparation for the indignities he had received when his heart was "exposed on the altars."[64] St. Margaret Mary pursued these practices. The feast, now transferred to the Friday after the feast of the Body and Blood of Christ, was celebrated locally by 1670, expanded throughout Europe in the coming decades, and extended to the whole church in 1856. The growing relationship between devotion to the Sacred Heart and Eucharist is manifest in the widespread practice of Benediction with Holy Hours and with Sacred Heart devotions. An association that became the Archconfraternity of the Holy Hour was established in 1829, centered at the Visitation Convent where Margaret Mary lived and is buried.[65] This Sacred Heart–eucharistic connection also helped generate the feast of the Eucharistic Heart of Jesus, established in 1921.

Prayer before the reserved Sacrament already occurred during the Middle Ages. Forty Hours Devotions, Benediction and Holy Hours were privileged variations on this ritual. New in this post-Tridentine era was the cultivation of visits to the Blessed Sacrament outside these treasured rituals; numerous devotional books promoted such visits. Already by 1580, the Spanish Carthusian Andrew Capella had published a three-part *Manual of Spiritual Exercises,* urging readers to visit the Blessed Sacrament whenever possible; by 1625 this popular work had been translated and made its way into the underground Catholic community in England.[66]

Few voices were as influential here as St. Alphonsus Liguori (d. 1787). His *Visits to the Most Blessed Sacrament and the Blessed Virgin Mary* has gone through more than two thousand editions in thirty-nine languages since first appearing in 1745.[67] In this concise work, he introduces the importance of visits to the "Most Holy Sacrament" and the "Most Blessed Virgin" while instructing the reader how to make a visit and engage in spiritual communion. Alphonsus then provides thirty-one brief guides, one for each day of the month, a short theological reflection, a prayer, and a final "aspiration," for example, "My Jesus, I will love only you."[68] Liguori's work well captures the spirituality and fervor behind this movement. Pius IX (d. 1878) named Liguori a Doctor of the Church and granted special indulgences for saying Liguori's prayers.

Vatican II and Beyond

In many respects, the remainder of this volume will be an exploration of the theologies, practices, and spiritualities surrounding eucharistic adoration and its parallel devotions since the Second Vatican Council (1962–65). Without preempting these explorations, there are yet notable historical developments that need to be signaled here.

Constitution on the Sacred Liturgy: The pivotal event for consideration of any liturgical practices in this period begins with Vatican II's 1963 *Constitution on the Sacred Liturgy* (*CSL*). This document articulates a fresh theological and spiritual understanding of worship and calls for reforms that properly align with this renewed vision. Furthermore, *CSL* is significant as a "roadmap" for all the council's work. Massimo Faggioli stresses that *CSL* does not simply instruct us how to shape reformed worship but is also a rich ecclesiological document for envisioning how to shape a reformed church.[69] In that spirit, Faggioli contends that *CSL* is an "intertextual document" that lies "at the crossroads of the whole corpus of Vatican II."[70]

This liturgical constitution devotes one brief paragraph to popular devotions (13) and mentions such devotions in only one other paragraph (17). The council highly recommends popular devotions, establishing the criteria that 1) they harmonize with the liturgical seasons, 2) are in agreement with the sacred liturgy, 3) are in some way derived from it, and 4) lead the people back to the liturgy. The rationale behind these guides is summarized in *CSL*'s affirmation that "the liturgy by its very nature is far superior to any of them" (13). Some have suggested that a fuller instruction on the nature of popular devotions and directives for negotiating the dynamics between the official liturgy of the church and popular devotions was significant unfinished business left by the council.

Mysterium Fidei: Even before the close of Vatican II, Pope St. Paul VI issued the 1965 encyclical *Mysterium Fidei* (The Mystery of Faith). Having written in response to what he considered serious pastoral concerns and anxiety, and to correct false opinions and practices, Paul VI believed that the restoration of the liturgy needed to be linked to eucharistic devotion, which he strongly endorsed (9, 64). He specifically mentioned exposition and processions of the Blessed Sacrament (56), the feast of *Corpus Christi* (63), and visits to the Blessed Sacrament (66).

Instruction on Eucharistic Worship: A more complete treatment of eucharistic devotions after the council is found in the Sacred Congregation of Rites' 1967 *Instruction on Eucharistic Worship.* The final ten sections (58–67) of that document provide directives for enacting various devotions. Many of these directives and theological explanations were incorporated into the more comprehensive Holy Communion and Worship of the Eucharist outside Mass. The 1967 document emphasizes the relationship between practices such as exposition and the Mass (60). Underscoring the centrality of the Mass, this document forbids celebrating Mass before the exposed sacrament (61), thus ending the previously approved practice of *Missa in coram Sanctissimo Sacramentum.*

Holy Communion and Worship of the Eucharist outside Mass:
Regarding eucharistic devotion, no postconciliar publication
is more important than the 1973 Holy Communion and Worship of the Eucharist outside Mass. Nathan Mitchell has under-
scored the groundbreaking nature of this document which, for
the first time, drew together in a single piece all relevant texts,
rites, and rubrics.[71] Chapter 2 of this document directly addresses worship of the Eucharist outside of Mass. Building on
the foundations laid by *CSL*, it draws liberally and often quotes
verbatim the 1967 *Instruction on Eucharistic Worship*, especially
its theological introduction (79–81) emphasizing how eucharistic adoration should draw the faithful into "deeper participation in the paschal mystery." While the 1973 document does
not treat extraliturgical forms of devotion such as visits to the
Blessed Sacrament, it does address "prayer before Christ the
Lord sacramentally present," noting that such practices extend
the union experienced in physical communion (81). Its introduction to eucharistic exposition pointedly notes that this practice cannot in anyway obscure Christ's desire to be with us as
food, medicine, and comfort in the Eucharist (82), reminiscent
of the comments of Nicholas of Cusa noted above. Like its 1967
predecessor, the 1973 document exhibits caution about "lengthy
exposition," which ordinarily should take place only once a
year (86). More extended exposition is possible for grave reasons with permission (87). Consonant with *CSL*'s emphasis on
active participation as a hallmark of the reform (14), there is a
consistent concern that there be suitable numbers of the faithful
present for any lengthy exposition of the sacrament (86). Such
exposition should not continue when there is a case of "too
few worshipers" (88). When it comes to adoration in religious
communities, however, having one or two members of the
community take turns before the Blessed Sacrament is allowed
and commended (90). When it comes to eucharistic processions, the 1973 document embraces Pope St. John XXIII's concern for reading the signs of the times. Like its 1967 antecedent,

it calls local ordinaries to judge whether public processions are "opportune in today's circumstances," recognizing that eucharistic processions do not qualify as some universal good, as they could contribute to a "loss of reverence to the sacrament" (101).

Pope St. John Paul II: Early into his pontificate, John Paul II issued the 1980 apostolic letter *Dominicae Cenae* (For Holy Thursday). Not unlike Paul VI in *Mysterium Fidei*, John Paul II wished to correct misunderstandings and even abuses related to the celebration of the Eucharist. Most important for our purposes is the letter's emphasis on adoration. The pope lifts up virtually every practice of adoration in the Catholic repertoire: prayer before the Blessed Sacrament; hours of adoration; short, prolonged, and annual exposition; Benediction; eucharistic processions; eucharistic congresses; and the feast of the Body and Blood of Christ (3). Throughout his pontificate, he will return to this theme. His 1994 letter to the archbishop of Seville is an appropriate summary of this concern when the pope writes, "I would like to repeat my invitation to you to make adoration of the Blessed Sacrament a habitual practice in all Christian Communities."[72]

During the pontificate of John Paul II, the church experienced a resurgence of eucharistic adoration, especially a growing interest in perpetual adoration. Indicative of this trend was the Pontifical Council of the Laity's approval of the statutes of the Association of Perpetual Eucharistic Adoration as a "universal and international public association of the faithful."[73] According to that council's own directory, there is also a recognized federation of Nocturnal Adoration Societies, which at last count included 39 associations representing 36 countries.[74] Questions around perpetual adoration in the United States prompted the United States Catholic Conference of Bishops' liturgy committee to make an official inquiry to the Vatican in 1995 regarding the appropriateness of this practice in parishes. In the wake of the Vatican response, some dioceses published directives for perpetual adoration, which is allowed only with the permission of the bishop.

Directory on Popular Devotions: Almost 40 years after the *Constitution on the Sacred Liturgy*, in 2001 the Vatican filled a notable gap with the *Directory on Popular Piety and the Liturgy: Principles and Guidelines*.[75] This comprehensive guide to the church's teaching on popular devotion recognizes this lacuna when it expresses its desire to ensure that such forms of piety "are not overlooked, nor their useful contribution to living in unity with Christ, in the Church, be forgotten" (1). The directory makes multiple contributions, including its attempts to offer definitions of terms such as *pious exercise* (7), *devotions* (8), *popular piety* (9), and *popular religiosity* (10). Its stress on the primacy of the church's official liturgy (11) and many useful instructions about inculturation, the values in popular piety (61–64), and general principles (75) will be revisited in the forthcoming chapter on theology. The relevant sections on eucharistic devotions are not extensive. Most attention is given to the Solemnity of the Body and Blood of Christ (160–63) and a few paragraphs on eucharistic adoration (164–65). Neither of these sections presents anything new, but both are useful summaries of previous teachings and directives.

Summary

The history of eucharistic adoration is quite complex and diverse. It has been a rich and enduring practice across Christianity and Roman Catholicism in particular. Later we will try to parse some of the theologies and spiritualities behind these practices. Suffice it to say that these various practices respond to a diversity of personal and ecclesial needs in varying contexts and cultures that continue to manifest themselves in the present age. Their flourishing seems to confirm in practice what the church announces in its official theologies: the liturgy, especially the Eucharist, is the fount and summit of the church's life (*CSL* 10). Eucharistic devotions are honored preparations for and extensions of the eucharistic liturgy.

Chapter Two

Theologizing about Eucharistic Devotions

Starting with the Liturgy

Our opening excursion into the history of adoration and other eucharistic practices outside of Mass provides invaluable background for understanding and framing parallel devotions today. As history demonstrates, much of the theologizing that provided the context for eucharistic devotions as they emerged in the Middle Ages centered on controversies concerning the nature of Christ's presence in the Eucharist. While these were and are important theological issues, they were a clear departure from the more ancient approach of theologizing from the liturgical action itself. That approach is well capsulized in the celebrated phrase of Prosper of Aquitaine (d. about 465), "the law of praying establishes the law of believing." A premiere example of this venerable form of theologizing is embedded in a sermon of St. Augustine, who explains the mystery of the Eucharist by drawing upon the rituals of baptism and the essential act of Communion. While he does cite two verses from St. Paul's writings, the bishop of Hippo spends much more time exegeting the actions that surround the Communion ritual. He writes:

So now if you want to understand the body of Christ,
listen to the Apostle Paul speaking to the faithful: You are
the body of Christ, member for member. If you, therefore,
are Christ's body and members, it is your own mystery
that is placed on the Lord's table! It is your own mystery
that you are receiving! You are saying Amen to what you
are—your response is a personal signature, affirming
your faith. When you hear "The Body of Christ" you reply
"Amen." Be a member of Christ's body, then, so that your
Amen may ring true! . . . When you received exorcism,
you were ground. When you were baptized, you were
leavened. When you received the first of the Holy Spirit,
you were baked. Be what you see; receive what you are.[1]

One of the hallmarks of the twentieth-century liturgical
reform was a return to the liturgical event as a fundamental
source for theologizing about the sacraments. Rather than rely-
ing upon philosophical concepts such as substance and acci-
dents, which were central to medieval debates about the
Eucharist, the rituals and their actual performance became
prized theological resources. This shift is sometimes framed
as a turn toward a theology *of* and *from* the liturgy—that is, a
properly liturgical theology—rather than a more abstract theology *about* sacraments apart from their ritual enactment.

This reorientation back to the church's official liturgy as the
determinant authority for pondering the doctrinal foundations
for popular devotions is enshrined in the *Constitution on the
Sacred Liturgy* (CSL). As referenced earlier, its brief consideration of popular devotion teaches that

such devotions should be so drawn up that they harmonize with the liturgical seasons, accord with the sacred
liturgy, are in some way derived from it, and lead the
people to it, since in fact the liturgy by its very nature is
far superior to any of them. (13)

This magisterial teaching has been consistently invoked in
the ensuing decades as the guiding principle for shaping and

enacting popular devotions for Roman Catholics. When it comes to eucharistic practices and devotions outside of Mass, this means that any appropriate theology for these rituals must similarly turn to the theology embedded in the celebration of the Mass itself. The conciliar constitution is clear that while all official liturgy is the fount and summit of the church's life, this is above all true of the Eucharist (*CSL* 10). Consequently, we must look to the actions and texts of the Mass as well as the dogmatic teaching drawn from them as the most trustworthy guide for shaping a doctrinally sound theology of any expanded eucharistic cult.

There are innumerable aspects of the eucharistic sacrifice that could direct these reflections. As we cannot possibly exhaust every aspect of this central mystery, there is a need to limit our focus. Consequently, we will concentrate on five key theological aspects of the eucharistic liturgy that find deep resonance in contemporary magisterial church teaching. These theological aspects will find complementary parallels in the next chapter when we consider the spirituality of eucharistic devotions outside of Mass.

The Christological Center

It has been common in the liturgical movement of the twentieth century and the ensuing reforms to talk about liturgy as "the work of the people." This unofficial definition is derived from the Greek word for *liturgy*, which is composed of two root elements. The Greek *leitos* means "public" or "belonging to the people." *Ergon* is the other Greek building block, translated as "work," especially a "work of duty or necessity." The combination of these two root words has often led folk to define liturgy as a public work or, more facilely, the work of the people.

There is deep wisdom in that definition that we will consider later under the rubric of the ecclesial nature of eucharistic worship. At the same time, however, there are at least two key problems with this somewhat reductionist definition. The first is that in ancient Greece the term *leitourgia* was not simply some visible form of labor. Someone repairing their family cottage or farming their own land was not involved in *leitourgia*. Rather, *leitourgia* was an ordinarily taxing endeavor—both time consuming and usually performed at one's own financial expense—clearly intended for the public good. Thus, *leitourgia* was not so much a work *of* the people, but rather a work performed *for the sake* of the people. This insight will contribute to our forthcoming consideration of the missiological nature of the eucharistic liturgy.

A more basic problem with attempting to define liturgy through any unnuanced translation of the root Greek words is that it renders the liturgy in general, and the Eucharist in particular, as a fundamentally human activity. This "work of the people" approach intimates that worship occurs first and foremost because of our initiation and hard work. That is not only wrong but actually borders on the heretical. It is undeniably true that human beings are summoned to participate fully in the liturgy (*CSL* 14). Thus, to a certain extent, liturgy is appropriately understood as an authentically human activity. It is also true that one of the key purposes of the liturgy—deeply embedded in the church's teaching—is for the sanctification of people. Consequently, worship is not simply an act of adoration to God but is also mutually beneficial to God's people (*CSL* 10). The baptized are true actors and even subjects of the liturgy, according to the Second Vatican Council (*CSL* 7), who engage in worship for their own sanctification. These are topics to which we will also return. However, from the outset it is necessary to clarify that neither the faithful nor the priest-presider is the initiating actor in the liturgical action. Liturgy is not principally our work. When turning back to the *Constitution on the Sacred Liturgy*, we find this doctrine announced in unambiguous language: "every liturgical celebration . . . is an action of Christ the priest and of his body, which is the church" (7).

Liturgically, this foundational truth is made explicit in the very structure of our collects and orations, continuously and appropriately offered "through Christ, our Lord." Furthermore, in the midst of the great thanksgiving we call the eucharistic prayer, before invoking the power of the Holy Spirit over the elements, the church acknowledges that the very celebration of these sacred mysteries is offered at Christ's command (Eucharistic Prayer III). The Second Eucharistic Prayer for Reconciliation is eloquent in professing Christ's determinative action in our salvation: "He himself is the Word that brings salvation, the hand you extend to sinners, the way by which your peace is offered to us." This is why the church is even able to celebrate "the reconciliation Christ has brought us." As a summary of this christological initiative, every eucharistic prayer culminates in an ancient doxology proclaiming that all glory and honor are offered to God through, with and in Christ. In these and multiple other ways, the reformed rites make it crystal clear that Eucharist is not a work achieved primarily through the inventiveness of the clergy or the earnestness of the baptized. Rather, it belongs to "the firstborn of all creation" (Col 1:15). Without the eternally preemptive action of the divine Logos, human beings would not even be capable of engaging in any form of eucharistic or sacramental worship.

This christological starting point reminds us that the agenda for all eucharistic action—whether the Mass, Benediction, or adoration—is a Christ agenda. The eucharistic liturgy as our premier school of discipleship unfolds this curriculum through its treasury of prayers, blessings, admonitions, and ritual gestures. Another honored source for this kingdom syllabus is the cycle of readings that traverse the church year as well as informed and thoughtful preaching on those texts. The Christ in Word and sacrament, uniquely revealed in eucharistic prayers and gospel proclamations, is the unerring litmus test for shaping and evaluating all eucharistic devotion.

The Paschal Mystery

One of the first implications of this christological turn is an invitation to embrace the essentially paschal character of all liturgy and every devotion authentically derived from it. The most common way Roman Catholics acknowledge this paschal reality is through our traditional language of "the sacrifice of the Mass." The Mass as a sacrifice is frequently explained by juxtaposing what happens at the altar with what happened at Jesus' crucifixion on Calvary. The sixteenth-century Council of Trent distinguished, somewhat graphically, between the "bloody manner" in which Christ offered himself on the cross and the "unbloody manner" in which that same sacrifice is freshly realized in every Mass (Session 22:2). Thus, the eucharistic liturgy is not simply an exercise in historical memory about the death of the Lord but is instead a full and dynamic engagement with all of the grace and saving power of that once-and-for-all saving event (Heb 7:27).

More recently, the understanding of this center of Christian liturgy has appropriately expanded to include not only the death of the Lord but also his passion, resurrection, and ascension. This broader image of the paschal mystery can be traced back to the writings of the second-century bishop Melito of Sardis. It gained renewed prominence during the twentieth-century liturgical movement, especially through the work of the liturgical pioneer Odo Casel (d. 1948). A Benedictine monk, Casel spoke about the "mystery-in-the-present" as a way to explain how a saving act like Christ's death is made present through our contemporary rites. By participating in the liturgy, the baptized not only recall but actually participate in Christ's salvific action. Casel's ground-breaking work clearly influenced Vatican II. This is evidenced by the repeated use of the language of paschal mystery throughout the documents of that council. The *Constitution on the Sacred Liturgy* seriously embraced this theme, and the language of paschal or paschal mystery occurs a dozen times in that document. Here is one key passage from this magisterial teaching:

> This work of human redemption and perfect glorification of God, foreshadowed by the wonders which God performed among the people of the Old Testament, Christ the Lord completed principally in the paschal mystery of his blessed passion, resurrection from the dead, and glorious ascension, whereby "dying, he destroyed our death and rising, restored our life." (5)

Following this teaching, the reformed Order of Mass under Pope St. Paul VI (d. 1978) inserted into the ancient Roman Canon (and into every other newly crafted eucharistic prayer) an acclamation proclaiming this "Mystery of Faith." The first acclamation to appear in the Sacramentary approved for use in the United States in 1974 is both a memorable and appropriate summary of the dynamic nature of this mystery: "Christ has died, Christ is risen, Christ will come again." The *Catechism of the Catholic Church* aptly summarizes, "In the liturgy of the Church, it is principally his own Paschal mystery that Christ signifies and makes present" (1085).[2]

This paschal center of the liturgy provides a foundation for all eucharistic devotion. The Vatican's 2001 *Directory on Popular Piety and the Liturgy* makes dozens of references to this core teaching. In critiquing past devotions, it notes that at certain stages of their evolution some pious practices of the people often "lacked a sufficient emphasis on the centrality of the Paschal mystery of Christ, foundation and summit of all Christian worship, and its privileged expression on Sunday" (41; cf. 48). When that directory turns to a specific consideration of eucharistic devotion, it instructs that two basic principles must be integrated into all such practices:

- the supreme reference point for Eucharistic devotion is the Lord's Passover; the Pasch as understood by the Fathers, is the feast of Easter, while the Eucharist is before all else the celebration of Paschal Mystery or of the Passion, Death and Resurrection of Christ;

- all forms of Eucharistic devotion must have an intrinsic reference to the Eucharistic Sacrifice, or dispose the faithful for its celebration, or prolong the worship which is essential to that Sacrifice. (161)

The significance of this paschal center is both profound and wide ranging. Some of these ramifications are decidedly pastoral, and we will later explore their implications for pastoral practice as well as for an authentic eucharistic spirituality. Before that, however, we need to articulate some theological foundations that will undergird those further reflections. One of them is recognizing that, as St. Thomas Aquinas argues, Jesus' sacrifice was offered in his human nature (*Summa Theologiae*, III, q. 48, a. 3). Jesus' death on Calvary was not some divine illusion but a completely enfleshed reality firmly planted within the created world. Like his birth, Jesus' death was a wholly incarnational act. Recognizing the thoroughly embodied events at the center of this mystery—the scourging, carrying of the cross, public disrobing, nailing, piercing with a lance, removal, and burial of the physical body—will demand a similarly embodied paschal spirituality.

A second theological insight brings us to a proper definition of *sacrifice* in paschal mode. Sacrifice was the defining practice of the Temple in Jerusalem at the time of Jesus. These rituals followed the sacrifice code outlined in the book of Leviticus. The ritual killing and burning of a wide variety of animals—as well as offerings of incense, grains, olive oil and salt—was the linchpin of Temple worship. When it comes to the "sacrifice" of Jesus on the Cross, however, we are dealing with an altogether different and completely unique event. The animals and elements in Israel's ritual sacrifices did not choose to die, nor in any way did they individually collaborate in the act. They were unwilling, even resistant participants. Jesus, on the other hand, was not an unwitting or uncompliant being. Rather, he freely and intentionally chose to die for our sake. We acknowledge this truth each Sunday when proclaiming the creed. As Nathan Mitchell evocatively summarizes, "Jesus became a 'living sacrifice' not because of what his tormentors did (which was homicide), but because of what he did (which was self-surrender in trust and love)."[3]

This realization brings us to an ancient truth about sacrifice that echoes throughout the Old Testament and is wholly magnified in the New Testament. The defining element of authentic sacrifice is not any physical destruction but a turning of the heart. The so-called sacrifice of Abraham (Gen 22:1-18), which Jewish scholars considered the epitome of sacrifice in the Hebrew Scriptures, does not have the death of Isaac at its center. Rather, the whole episode pivots on the faithfulness of Abraham. God was appeased not because of some blood-letting but because of the heart-rending of this revered religious forebear. Thus, the psalmist could proclaim that true sacrifice is a contrite heart (Ps 51:17). Parallel passages through the Old Testament affirm that God's delight is not in burnt offerings but obedience (1 Sam 15:22). The prophet Micah is particularly powerful in his rebuke of extravagant offers of sacrifice, even including the sacrificing of one's own child or person. Instead, the prophet clearly articulates what God requires: "to do justice, and to love kindness, and to walk humbly with your God" (Mic 6:8).

The immolation of Jesus on the altar of Calvary was the visible sacrament of the invisible mystery of God's love that had animated Jesus' generosity throughout his entire public ministry. His sacrifice did not begin on Golgotha. Rather, all of his teachings and healings, the wrestling with demons and struggles with opponents—sometimes including his own disciples—were each in their own way paschal seeds that blossomed in all of their terrible beauty on the cross. Strikingly, such sustained pouring out of self was never self-serving. Jesus did not practice ascetic practices or put himself forward as a martyr for the sake of his own holiness or personal salvation. He was already the very definition of holiness and the source of salvation. Rather, his heroic martyrdom was always and eternally for others. His very incarnation was irrevocable proof that God had a love affair with humanity (John 4:16) and would deny nothing—including the death of the firstborn—to confirm that love.

In the culminating act of this lifetime of reflective selfless-ness, Jesus chose with eyes wide open to be betrayed, humili-ated, scourged, and nailed to a cross. His complete surrender in love to the one he called Abba and his willingness to pour himself out for humanity marked not only his death but his whole earthy existence. It is the sustained totality of this self-giving that takes us to the heart of the "mystery of faith." In a similar way, the paschal summons of every eucharistic devo-tion calls for more than awe or gratitude in contained moments of adoration. Instead, it summons the baptized, in all of our inadequacies, to live a similarly sacrificial life poured out for others.

Ecclesial Praying

Evidence from both the past and the present suggests that for many across the ages, eucharistic devotion has become a highly personal, even private event. For example, the intense reflections of a mystic such as Mechthild of Magdeburg, ref-erenced in the previous chapter, reveals a privileged intimacy between this holy woman and the Christ, accentuating a par-ticular relationship that is not posited of other believers.

This does not mean that all advocates of eucharistic devo-tion considered such practices only as an avenue to a personal relationship with God. St. Juliana of Liège's quest for a feast in honor of Christ's Body and Blood—clearly born from her own eucharistic devotion—demonstrates an admirable sensitivity for the liturgical integrity of the whole church. Despite this shining example and that of many others like her, acts of popular piety in general, and those surrounding eucharistic devotion in particular, often ceded primacy to what the *Directory on Popular Piety and the Liturgy* frames with the language of "subjectivity" (34). Such devotions, according to that directory, oriented the faithful "towards a certain type of individual piety which accentuates detachment from the world and the invitation to hear the Master's voice interiorly. Less attention is devoted to the communitarian and ecclesial aspects of prayer and to liturgical spirituality" (35). This orientation toward the interior and intensely personal was understandable in times such as the Middle Ages when there was so much emphasis on the need to save one's own soul from eternal damnation or at least limit the time one might need to spend in purgatory.

The reforms of the twentieth century witnessed a revolution in understandings of what it means to be church and particularly a church at worship. Many of these developments appear in the *Dogmatic Constitution on the Church*. Along with the more traditional view of the church as hierarchical (chap. 3), these renewed images included the church as the people of God (chap. 2), the church as the body of Christ (7–8), the church as a sacrament (1, 9, 48), and the church as communion (1, 50–51). What is notable about all these reformed images is their shared communitarian overtones. This is distinctly true when imaging church as a communion, a metaphor that rose to great prominence in the extraordinary Roman Synod of 1985. While there are many ways of thinking about the church as communion, all of them emphasize church as a collective "we" and not simply as something residing in an elite cadre of prelates or even the pope.

The reformed Order of Mass, long before the 1985 synod, reflected this communitarian theology. One of the distinguishing characteristics of the 1969 rite for celebrating Mass promulgated under Pope St. Paul VI was its use of plural pronouns. At the very outside of that rite, after the sign of the cross and the greeting, the options for either the rite of blessing and sprinkling with holy water (option A) or the multiple ways of celebrating the penitential rite (option B) are dominated by the language of "us" and "we." This collective language pervades the new Order of Mass.

While the Tridentine Rite of 1570 may be far removed from current memory or experience, a comparison of the language in its texts with those of the 1969 rite provides a quite stark contrast. One of the most extraordinary illustrations of their difference comes by comparing the prayers of the "offertory" in the 1570 rite with its parallel "preparation of the altar and the gifts" in the 1969 rite. The opening prayers in each of these liturgies are sufficient to make the point:

1570	1969
Accept, O holy Father, almighty and eternal God, this spotless host, which I your unworthy servant, offer to you, my living and true God, for my own countless sins, transgressions, and failings; for all here present and for all faithful Christians, both living and dead: that it may profit both me and them salvation to life everlasting.	Blessed are you, Lord God of all creation. Through your goodness we have this bread to offer, which earth has given and human hands have made. It will become for us the bread of life. (Response): Blessed be God for ever.

In the language and theology of the 1570 rite, it is the priest who is the primary actor. He is the one who offers the sacrifice, first for himself and then for others. This and similar texts make it clear that in the Tridentine Mass, the priest was not only the primary but also the sole actor in the rite. The language of the 1969 text is striking not only because of the change from the singular to the plural—from "I" to "we"—but also because the critical participation of the assembly in this action is confirmed by their repeated "Blessed be God for ever." The ecclesial body of Christ is clearly a subject of this worship through the initiative of the head of that body, Jesus Christ. The assembly in the Tridentine offertory, on the other hand, was silent in this pivotal moment, which was the first part of the Mass the baptized were required to attend in order to fulfill their Sunday obligation.

Innumerable other examples from the reformed Order of Mass could be cited to confirm the fundamentally ecclesial nature of reformed eucharistic worship. Such texts are ritual validations of the previously cited text from Vatican II that acknowledges liturgy as an "action of Christ the priest and of his body, which is the church" (*CSL* 7). This truth finds a dramatic affirmation in the *General Instruction of the Roman Missal* and its official explanation of the dynamics of the eucharistic prayer: the very heart of our eucharistic worship. That document clearly states, "[T]he meaning of this Prayer is that the whole congregation of the faithful joins with Christ in confessing the great deeds of God and in the offering of Sacrifice" (78). While the priest speaks the prayer out loud, he does so "in the name of the entire community" and not simply on his own behalf (78). Thus, in the repositioned offering—removed from the preparation of the gifts and now planted firmly in the eucharistic prayer—the "I offer" language of the 1570 rite is gone. Instead, the potent phrase "we offer" is consistently repeated across the eucharistic prayers crafted for the reformed liturgy.

Eucharistic worship is neither private nor the action of a sole individual. Conspicuously, the *General Instruction of the Roman Missal* does not provide any rubrics for a private Mass but only a "Mass at which only one minister participates." This instruction also establishes that private Mass and "Mass at which only one minister participates" are not synonyms, for the latter is defined as one "celebrated by a Priest with only one minister to assist him and to make the responses" (252). The exceptional situation in which a priest is allowed to celebrate Mass without a minister or at least one member of the faithful is allowed only "for a just and reasonable cause" (254). On the other hand, the Tridentine Rite not only recognized that a Mass celebrated by a priest alone was allowed, but it was actually the foundational model for that rite. From the viewpoint of the church's law at the time, such a private Mass was both allowed and acknowledged as completely acceptable: canonical language describes such a Mass as both "licit" and "valid." The reforms of Vatican II and the eucharistic liturgy of 1969 reflecting those reforms no longer take the private Mass as a norm of any kind. The liturgy emanating from the council—like the council itself—is a thoroughly ecclesial act. A recent affirmation of this position came from a 2021 letter from the Vatican Secretariat of State that banned the daily private celebration of Masses at none other than St. Peter's Basilica.

The Missionary Move

For many, the language of "mission" or "evangelization" summons images of intrepid zealots setting sail for distant lands, or at least brave believers visiting unexplored neighborhoods on a quest to find converts. This caricature of the foreign or domestic missionary was fairly accurate for centuries and may yet be true today in some contexts. Over the past few decades, however, missiologists have evolved different understandings of specific missionary activities and, more importantly, about the core identity of the church as a missionary venture.

A phrase that epitomized this evolution, developed by the missiologist David Bosch (d. 1992), is that of *missio Dei* ("The mission of God"). Bosch's basic insight was that mission is not so much a work of the church as an attribute of God. The God revealed in Jesus Christ is a "missionary God."[4] This revolution in thought prompted the now widely accepted maxim by Catholic-Christian missiologists and other theologians that it is not so much that the church has a mission, but that God's mission has a church. As Roman Catholic theologians Stephen Bevans and Roger Schroeder summarize, the *missio Dei* is "the very mission of God in creation, redemption and continual sanctification."[5]

The teachings of the Second Vatican Council, which deeply influenced Bosch's theology, clearly point us in the same direction. For example, the opening paragraph of the *Dogmatic Constitution on the Church* speaks about the church not only as a sign but also as an instrument of communion with God and the unity of the whole human race (1). The vision of church here is for the benefit of both the faithful and the entire world. Thus, the document confirms that the church has a "universal mission." The Johannine text about God's love affair with the world (John 4:16) quickly comes to mind here. An even more potent teaching from Vatican II on the missionary character of the church is found in a document that is unfortunately seldom read, particularly by those concerned with worship and devotion. The *Decree on the Church's Missionary Activity* clearly teaches that "the church on earth is by its very nature missionary" (2).

Although they constitute the briefest section in the Order of Mass, the Concluding Rites amply summarize the missionary core of the Christian life. The ancient imperative to "go forth" (*Ite*) is not simply a dismissal. Rather it is a ritual announcement of the great commission to "[g]o . . . and make disciples of all nations" (Matt 28:19). The current eucharistic liturgy amplifies that ancient instruction with texts that charge the baptized to proceed out into the world, glorifying the Lord with their lives, and enjoins them in their leaving to announce the gospel of the Lord.

This commissioning is not an abrupt signal for folk to leave, but a ritual summary of the multiple missionary prompts that have been rehearsed throughout the eucharistic liturgy. During the preceding liturgy, the faithful have been gathered for a purpose and summoned to respond to God's Word. We have been invited into praise and belief in a God who sent the Only Begotten on his world-altering mission. We have been called into reconciliation and urged to share peace, while simultaneously invited into communion with God, the whole of creation, and all humankind. Thus, at this final commissioning we are poised to be launched into the world and fulfill our vocation rehearsed at the very center of the eucharistic prayer:

> Open our eyes
> to the needs of our brothers and sisters;
> inspire in us words and actions
> to comfort those who labor and are burdened.
> Make us serve them truly,
> after the example of Christ and at his command.
> And may your Church stand as a living witness
> to truth and freedom,
> to peace and justice,
> that all people may be raised up to a new hope.
> (Eucharistic Prayer IV for Various Needs)

So many texts in today's Order of Mass affirm the expansive and generous energy of the eucharistic liturgy. Solemn blessings pray that the community be made "a light for your brothers and sisters" (Epiphany) and "effective in good works" (Ordinary Time IV). Multiple orations ask that the faithful might

- "display the gentleness of your charity in the service of our neighbor" (feast of St. Francis de Sales)

- "work for justice among the poor and the oppressed" (feast of St. Katharine Drexel)

- "share our food with the hungry" (feast of St. Isidore)
- "become peacemakers" (feast of St. Elizabeth of Portugal)
- "love our neighbor in deeds and in truth" (feast of St. Peter Claver),
- respond "to the needs of the world today" (feast of Blessed Marie Rose Durocher),
- "not be afraid to lay down our life for others" (feast of St. Josaphat),
- "serve with unfailing charity the needy and those afflicted" (feast of St. Elizabeth of Hungary), and
- share God's "gifts in loving service" (Thanksgiving Day).

This missiological vector, so clearly confirmed in the prayers and actions of the Mass, is repeatedly endorsed in magisterial teachings and eucharistic practices. For example, in 2000, Pope St. John Paul II recognized that "the celebration of the Eucharist, the Sacrament of the Lord's Passover, is in itself a missionary event."[6] That insight is reflected in the practices and directions of Eucharistic Congresses, which the Catholic Church has convened with such regularity since 1881. As Cardinal Peter Turksson has observed, "It is instructive . . . to notice how many of the themes are explicitly social or public . . . and how few, by contrast, are explicitly about Adoration, contemplative prayer, holiness, or spirituality."[7] Memorable for the United States was the Eucharistic Congress in Philadelphia on the two-hundredth anniversary of our country: the theme was "Eucharist and the Aspirations of the Human Family."

If the church is fundamentally missionary and if the Eucharist is the source and summit of the church's life and mission—

as recently reaffirmed by Pope Benedict XVI (b. 1927) in *Sacramentum Caritatis* (The Sacrament of Charity, 84)[8]—then it follows that such a missionary impulse must be integral to all eucharistic devotion. Speaking specifically about eucharistic adoration, Pope Benedict taught, "Far from being a privatized, ethereal devotion, as some fear, adoration is a basic posture in life. . . . Adoration must surely give rise to the service of neighbor."[9] If Eucharist commits us to the poor, as the *Catechism of the Catholic Church* asserts (1397), then all eucharistic devotion must do the same. Cardinal Luis Tagle sums this position up well in his reflection on authentic adoration in light of Jesus own passion and death:

> I hope that eucharistic adoration will lead us to recognize in Jesus the companion filled with compassion for the countless crucified victims of our days. May it let us also give time to these innumerable and innocent victims of our time. We should be able to touch the heart of Jesus who knew their tears and their sorrows because he lived with them and turned such tears and sorrow into seeds of hope for love. Considering the suffering of the other, we could become, like the centurion, bearers of truth and the heroes of faith. And I am hopeful that when people see how lovingly we know how to carry the cross of others, they too will be able to see the face of innocence and of the son of God in each of us.[10]

In his stirring apostolic exhortation *The Joy of the Gospel*,[11] Pope Francis (b. 1936) calls all the baptized to be missionary disciples, committed to a church that is permanently in a state of mission (120ff.) In that same exhortation, he affirms not only the importance of prayer, but specifically of adoration in order to maintain our zeal as missionary disciples. At the same time, he recognizes the problem that "some moments of prayer can become an excuse for not offering one's life in mission" (262). Just as the dynamic of our eucharistic liturgy is pointedly centrifugal, commissioning the baptized to go out into the world and witness to the joy and justice of Jesus, so must authentic eucharistic devotion have a similar missionary trajectory.

Eucharistic Ecology

Mentioning eucharistic devotion and ecology in the same sentence might strike some folk as at least odd, if not inappropriate. While Eucharist and its devotions are ancient Christian traditions, concerns about the environment could be dismissed as a contemporary fad or some New Age concern. Ironically, however, reverence for creation in the Judeo-Christian tradition—as well as an awareness that creation itself offers praise and adoration to God—is a tradition more ancient than even that of the Eucharist. For example, the psalms that so regularly punctuate Christian worship are filled with texts about heaven and earth, sun and moon, shining stars, and the waters above the heavens praising the Lord (Ps 148). One of the most fulsome of these Old Testament passages is the canticle from the book of Daniel in which everything from lightning and whales to birds and snow is called upon to offer cosmic praise to the Creator (Dan 3:57-82). The psalmist recognizes that entirely independently of human aid, all of creation praises God (Ps 19:1-4). Aside from the Old Testament, the New Testament reminds us that God is "above all and through all and in all" (Eph 4:6), that all creation waits in eager expectation for revelation (Rom 8:19), and that every creature in heaven, on earth, and in the sea offers praise and worship "[t]o the one seated on the throne and to the Lamb" (Rev 5:13).

These and a plethora of other biblical texts that wed creation to the God who called the whole of the cosmos into being and deemed it good (Gen 1), have deeply influenced Christian worship and its theology. Some may be surprised by the numerous references to creation and the notable ecological resonance that reverberates through the texts, gestures, and elements of the Mass. Even before pondering what is in our official liturgical books, we must reckon with the uninterrupted tradition of Christian worship that heartily embraces gifts drawn from the earth. Wheat, bread, and grape wine quickly come to mind, but we cannot forget the wax of bees, the oil from olives, water from the seas, incense from trees and plants, ashes from palms, stone from the earth, and the wood of the cross. Furthermore, where would our Northern Hemisphere Easter celebrations be without all of those lilies, or who imagines the festival of Christmas without a sanctuary bursting with fir trees and poinsettias? This is what theologians sometimes explain as the "catholic imagination." This pervasive imagination perceives God as both aligned with and easily revealed in the whole of creation. Such a catholic imagination affirms our deployment of these many splendors of creation in our official worship and devotions.

Then there are all those liturgical texts brimming with ecological references and creational resonance. The Belgian theologian Joris Geldhof has provided a rich and instructive overview of many of these. A few examples from the Roman Missal that Geldhof highlights include the blessing formula for Christmas in which the liturgical texts assert that through the incarnation God has joined earthly and heavenly things. Thus, from a theological perspective, the nativity of the Only Begotten has cosmic and not simply human ramifications. The second preface from the same feast confirms that Christ's coming in history not only restores the descendants of Adam and Eve but also restores the entirety of creation. Eucharistic Prayer III, echoing the psalmists we have previously referenced, notes that it is right and just that every creature praise God. Geldhof goes on to recall the insights of the celebrated Jesuit liturgist and musician Joseph Gelineau (d. 2008), who served as a theological expert at Vatican II. Commenting on the newly created Eucharistic Prayer IV that emerged after that council, Gelineau observed that this prayer—unlike any other before it—reflected a "cosmic sense."[12]

There is probably no part of the reformed Mass that day in and day out calibrates eucharistic worship to the created world more than the newly fashioned "preparation of the gifts and table." As noted above, this freshly shaped ritual moment in the liturgy does not focus on offering, which instead occurs at the heart of the eucharistic prayer (*General Instruction of the Roman Missal* 79). Instead, this transitional rite from the Liturgy of the Word to the eucharistic prayer, whose text in part is cited above (p. 46), is fundamentally marked by praise. Notice there is no intercession in this text or its companion prayer over the cup. Instead, this benediction brims with praise for the God of all creation who allows the gifts of the earth to be transformed through human collaboration to be the very stuff of the Eucharist.

Theologians across the centuries have pondered the importance of creation as both a reflection of its Creator as well as a pathway to discipleship and grace. One notable contemporary example is the British scientist-theologian Arthur Peacocke (d. 2006). In his powerful *Creation and the World of Science: The Re-Shaping of Belief*, Peacocke contends that is it absolutely appropriate for us to consider the natural world as a sacrament, because like any true sacrament it both reveals and effects. In its revelatory capacity, the natural world announces something essential about God as creator that we would not know without it. Beyond that, however, this created gift serves as a reliable vehicle for drawing human beings into praise and adoration of the Holy One who brought the cosmos into being.[13]

It is not only contemporary theologians, however, who make this creational move. One of the most celebrated examples of an ancient source of wisdom on this topic is St. Maximus the Confessor (d. 662), whom Pope Benedict XVI characterized as "the great Greek doctor of the Church."[14] Maximus's reflection is unique in the way that he characterizes creation as having a vocation. Ordinarily, we imagine that only people have vocations or a call from God. In the theological imagination of Maximus, however, creation was brought into existence so that it might reveal the Holy One and participate in the richness of God. According to Maximus, the whole of the cosmos praises God with silent voices. Since humans are joined to creation, our responsibility is to give that cosmic praise voice (*Quaestiones ad Thalassium* 51). Our human vocation joins with that of the cosmos in giving praise to the Creator. Thus, as the respected theologian John D. Zizioulas summarizes, "a human being is a priest of creation as he or she freely turns it into a vehicle of communion with God and fellow human beings."[15]

That priestly metaphor well characterizes the patron of my own religious community, St. Francis of Assisi (d. 1226), whom Pope St. John Paul II named the patron saint of ecology in 1979. Unofficially, others have dubbed him a "nature mystic" because of his deep appreciation of nature as an honored tool for channeling the presence of God.[16] Legends abound concerning the poor man of Assisi's oneness with creation, from his preaching to the birds to his crafting a pact between the wolf of Gubbio and the townspeople so that all might live in peace. More than these charming tales, however, Francis's "Canticle of Creation" reveals his profound ecological spirituality. Francis not only celebrated the created world as a source of constant praise to the Creator; he prayerfully aligned himself with creation as he recognized sun and moon, wind and water, fire and earth as sisters and brothers joining with him in a cosmic liturgy of praise. Although he was never formally ordained a priest, Francis was a true priest of creation. His priestly service here was embracing creation as a revered and honored source of communion with the entirety of the cosmos and the Holy One who brought them all into being. One of St. Francis's most celebrated followers, St. Bonaventure (d. 1274), further developed these perspectives by noting the intimate relationship between creation and the Trinity. As Ilia Delio summarizes, Bonaventure understood creation as a mirror that reflects the wisdom and goodness of the Triune God. More than that, however, Bonaventure understood creation as a "book" in which the Trinity both shines forth and is represented.[17] This image would find resonance in the ideas of Pope St. John Paul II and Pope Francis.

It is fitting that the patron of ecology's twenty-first–century namesake should take up this ecological spirituality with such enthusiasm and clarity. Certainly, Pope Francis is not the first pontiff to reflect theologically upon the gifts of creation. His encyclical *Laudato Si'*[18] is replete with citations especially from Pope Benedict XVI and Pope St. John Paul II. Building on their work and that of many others, Pope Francis develops the most comprehensive papal document ever written on creation and our responsibilities toward this incalculable gift. While Francis's writing here is not explicitly about Eucharist or sacraments, the pope does help us, in the section of that encyclical subtitled "On Care for Our Common Home," to regard the whole created universe as sacramental.

For example, Pope Francis teaches that "the entire universe speaks of God's love," and that everything from soil and water to mountains is, as it were, "a caress of God" (84). Thus, in the spirit of St. Bonaventure, creation can be understood as a precious book authored by God, and the letters in that book are "the multitude of created things present in the universe" (85). Drawing on Pope St. John Paul II, he stresses that alongside the revelation in Scripture, creation itself is a divine manifestation (85). Furthermore, Pope Francis not only speaks of the sacredness of the world, recognizing that nature reveals God, but he goes further in asserting that nature is actually a "locus" of God's presence (88). When Pope Francis explicitly speaks of sacraments, he notes that the seven sacraments of the church are a privileged way in which nature is taken up by God to become a "means of mediating supernatural life" (235).

Eucharistic devotions ordinarily presume some proximity to the reserved Blessed Sacrament, specifically the consecrated bread. Magisterial teaching instructs us that the transubstantiated elements are the true, real, and substantial presence of Christ. The consecrating transformation, however, does not obliterate nature. In perceiving the bread with our senses, we are reminded in the most wondrous of ways how nature is precisely taken up by God in order to mediate the Divine Presence and offer a pathway to eternal life. In the poetic musings of the Jesuit scientist and theologian Pierre Teilhard de Chardin (d. 1955), "the sacramental Species are formed by the totality of the world."[19] Thus, every eucharistic encounter invites the same praise for this created totality that resounds at the center of the prayers at the preparation of the gifts during Mass. Furthermore, just as every eucharistic devotion is an invitation to mission and discipleship in the world, so does every such devotion specifically summon us to become priests of creation, since created gifts are essential components of our entire sacramental system. Authentic eucharistic devotions must form us as reverent ministers of all created gifts and responsible stewards of the natural world, which is our necessary and unavoidable context for journeying into eternal life. Thus, in his reflections on an "earthly mysticism," the revered Jesuit theologian Karl Rahner (d. 1984) invites us to profess that Christ is at the very "heart of this earthly world and [is] the secret seal of its eternal validity."[20]

Summary

Contemporary church teaching insists that popular devotions need to be aligned to our official worship (*CSL* 13). Consequently, such teachings instruct that devotions should in some way be derived from the liturgy of the church and at the same time lead back to it. In order to craft a proper theology of any devotion, such a theology must similarly have an integral relationship to the liturgy, which is its source and summit. Throughout this chapter we have highlighted certain key theological foundations of the Mass—the pivotal eucharistic act of the church. We have also begun to illustrate how these theological foundations, embedded in the very rites and texts of the eucharistic Sacrifice, both illuminate eucharistic devotion and signal directions for an appropriate spirituality of eucharistic devotions and the pastoral implementation of such devotions. As we unfold these implications for an authentic eucharistic spirituality and pastoral implementation, we will continue to reference these liturgical-theological linchpins in order to provide an integrated and coherent view of eucharistic devotions in the wake of Vatican II.

Chapter Three

Facets of a Eucharistic Spirituality

Introduction

There are many concepts in religion that could vie for the mythical title of "God's most ambiguous idea." For Christians, the Trinity is certainly at the top of the list. No matter how we try to explain it, the mystery of the Trinity remains fundamentally beyond human perception and ultimately impenetrable. From my perspective, other major contenders for that title include the Immaculate Conception, Christ's descent into hell, and that unnamed yet unforgivable sin against the Holy Spirit mentioned in Mark's gospel (3:29).

At the level of lived belief, the concept of spirituality can be equally mystifying. Most Roman Catholics have not been catechized to understand the nature of spirituality, much less helped to understand that they actually have one. From time to time I have asked folk, "How would you describe your spirituality?" The consistent response is a blank stare, ordinarily followed by a request to explain. Some believe that only the very saintly are worthy of having anything close to a spirituality, which is consequently out of reach for ordinary Christians.

While the language of spirituality might summon images of esoteric knowing, or closely guarded secrets about the mystical life, the concept is actually quite simple. Our spirituality is basically the way in which we live out our relationship with God on a day-to-day basis. Quite often it is an unconscious or at least unexplored path. Beyond explicit religious activities such as going to Church or reciting prayers, it is our pattern of moving through the world and making meaning in the presence of God and in relationship to God's people. It encompasses the concrete ways in which we act out our faith.

There are people who do not profess any explicit belief in God who surprisingly enough also find the language of spirituality to be a useful framework. For many such humanists, agnostics, or even atheists, it operates as an alternative or substitute for institutional religion. It often is considered a modern form of sacredness, largely focused on the individual and oriented toward emotions and experiences rather than any religious norms or established belief systems.[1] For Christians, on the other hand, spirituality is a way to describe our vision of being human and making our way through life in the presence of a loving God, revealed in Jesus Christ, whose Spirit is active in the world and in our lives.

Some might be acquainted with the academic study of spirituality, where it is considered a specific theological discipline. The groundbreaking work of Sandra Schneiders[2] and others at the end of the twentieth century helped establish spirituality as a credible and rigorous way of doing theology. It is also possible to consider various religious communities or other groups to have established their own "schools" of spirituality. So, Jesuits can be said to have a distinctive Ignatian spirituality, drawn from the teachings and example of St. Ignatius of Loyola (d. 1556). A Benedictine spirituality is one that is reliant upon the masterful Rule of St. Benedict from the sixth century. Franciscans, on the other hand, could claim their own Franciscan spirituality patterned on the life and writings of St. Francis of Assisi. Most laity, however, do not study academic theology, nor do they necessarily follow the teachings or spiritual path of any particular saint. Rather, the lived spiritual life of most of the baptized is more eclectic and wide-ranging.

Obviously, there are many laudable and well-tested spiritualities available to Christians. It would be clearly inappropriate to suggest that one was more praiseworthy than another. At the same time, however, because of the enduring way the Roman Catholic Church prizes the Eucharist, it seems difficult for me to conceive of a Catholic spirituality that does not have a eucharistic hue or tonality. The church magisterially teaches that the liturgy—especially the Eucharist—is both the source and the summit of the whole of our ecclesial life together. As summarized in the *Constitution on the Sacred Liturgy*:

> The liturgy is the summit toward which the activity of the church is directed; it is also the source from which all its power flows. . . . From the liturgy, therefore, and especially from the Eucharist, grace is poured forth upon us as from a fountain, and our sanctification in Christ and the glorification of God to which all other activities of the church are directed, as toward their end, are achieved with maximum effectiveness. (10)

If the liturgy, especially the Mass, is such a central source of sanctification, it is reasonable to conclude that it should also be an unavoidable wellspring for the various spiritualities that mark our lives. This seems particularly important for those of us who regularly nourish our spiritual life with eucharistic devotions. Having a eucharistic spirituality, however, means more than frequently engaging in eucharistic practices. If a spirituality is the way we live our faith in the day to day unfolding of our lives, then a eucharistic spirituality means that those same lives are motivated and nourished by key spiritual aspects of the Eucharist itself.

In the previous chapter, we outlined some of the principal theological truths that are consistently celebrated in and communicated through the Mass. In a complementary way, this chapter will pair each of those theological insights with some key spiritual aspect of the eucharistic liturgy that can aid us in pursuing what the theologian Karl Rahner called the mysticism of everyday life.[3] Considering these spiritual aspects illustrates their deep interconnectedness with the theological aspects of the Eucharist we previously considered. Hopefully, this exploration will allow us to perceive more clearly how the many strands of our lived spiritualities are also interconnected, though sometimes in hidden and mysterious ways.

We will begin by revisiting the christological center of eucharistic theology and link it with a spirituality best described as embodied. The paschal facet of a eucharistic theology affirms that every parallel eucharistic spirituality is essentially sacrificial, which will be our second topic here. Next, we will reimagine the ecclesial character of eucharistic spirituality through a relational lens, particularly befriending neighbors and strangers. The missiological perspective allows us to ponder the pervasive yet surprising activity of God's spirit in the world, which both astonishes and humbles us. Finally, a spirituality rooted in a eucharistic ecology serves as an appropriate and integrating summary, embracing the interconnectedness of all life that at its core is reliant on the divine extravagance of a generous and loving God.

The Christological: Acknowledging Bodies

Eucharist does not happen without bodies. Jesus demonstrated this in the thoroughly incarnate way he modeled eucharistic dining throughout his earthly life. The pivotal Last Supper, for example, was not a "thought experiment" but a full enacted meal. It consisted of multiple courses of food and cups of wine, all prescribed by the Passover traditions which provided the context for this farewell meal. Besides these material gifts of the earth, every Seder meal included prescribed gestures, textual recitations, and ritual actions that Jewish tradition dictated and gospel witnesses confirm. Beyond these ancient elements, Jesus distinctly interpreted this embodied liturgy when he divested himself of his outer clothing, wrapped himself in a towel, poured water into a basin and washed his disciples' feet (John 13:4-5). In so doing, he symbolically transferred the ritual from a table filled with food stuffs to his own body. In this foot-washing service he announced himself as the incarnate Lamb: the traditional food at the center of a Passover meal. He was the Passover sacrifice, distinctly revealed in this act of humble service and soon to be rendered eternally memorable in his death on the cross.

Besides his climactic Last Supper, however, we cannot overlook the raft of earthly meals that both foreshadowed and ultimately led to that final gathering. The Gospel of Luke alone reports ten such table gatherings. Maybe even more telling than these multiple meal events is the repeated accusation announced across the gospels about this public feasting: Jesus ate and drank with sinners (Matt 9:11; Mark 2:16; Luke 5:30). As wondrously revealed in this table ministry, Jesus had so fully embraced and completely incorporated the created world and humanity into his divine self that he could mystically transfer his presence into a humble piece of bread and cup of wine.

Consonant with the pervasive table ministry of Jesus, the Christian celebration of the Eucharist throughout the ensuing centuries has remained a distinctly embodied event. Without fail, bodies gather, the Good News is audibly proclaimed, tangible fruits of the earth and work of human hands are gathered and brought forth, knees are bended and heads are lifted in prayer, beloved and stranger are embraced in the peace of Christ, bread is broken and shared, wine is poured and savored, and transubstantiated believers are commissioned back into the world. This pivotal practice of our faith at its core is an enfleshed event.

Even when livestreamed on Facebook, downloaded from YouTube, or otherwise digitally accessed—which millions did during the COVID-19 pandemic—these cybernated Eucharists still required bodies. As the Roman Catholic theologian Teresa Berger notes:

> Digitally mediated liturgical practices are material practices, as are all offline liturgies. In the case of digitally mediated worship, this material practice is enabled, foundationally, by the interface of a human body with a computer or other internet-accessing device. Digitally mediated practices of prayer and worship thus cannot be separated either from a physical body or from materiality. A simple example of this is the Cyber-Rosary available on the website of the cathedral of the Diocese of Bridgeport, Connecticut. The website instructs: "In this Cyber-Rosary, when it's time to pray on a rosary bead, click on the bead and it will change from blue to gold." The person praying, in other words, instead of moving beads, moves a cursor and clicks. The change in color indicates the bead has been prayed. . . . In short, it is clear that both online and offline praying involves human bodies and a range of other materialities.[4]

This indisputable evidence of the incarnate nature of sacraments in general and the eucharistic in particular points to a deep truth about Judeo-Christian revelation: God has chosen to be present to us through mediation. It is true that there are extraordinary revelations in the Old and New Testaments when God communicates directly with human beings without employing any intermediate elements or people. Thus, the prophet Ezekiel does have a vision of the likeness of God's glory (Ezek 1:28) and Exodus relates that the elders of Israel actually "saw the God of Israel" (Exod 24:10). The outstanding example of such a revelation in the New Testament concerns God's resounding announcement of the belovedness of Jesus, both at his baptism (e.g., Matt 3:17) as well as at his transfiguration (Luke 9:35). However, these were extraordinary events. Encountering the unmediated presence of God was not only unusual; it was considered dangerous. Thus, God said to Moses, "[Y]ou cannot see my face; for no one shall see me and live" (Exod 33:20). More common than direct visions of God is the Holy One's presence mediated through a burning bush (Exod 3:2-4), a pillar of fire by day or fire at night (Exod 13:21), or even a gentle breeze (1 Kgs 19:12). Most important of all such mediated presences is the incarnate Jesus Christ. In this wondrous mystery, God chose to communicate divinity through a human person. Christian faith teaches us that the face of this Palestinian Jew was at first a hidden reflection of the Creator of the universe. His divinity was not initially nor easily accessed through his humanity, and many not only rejected him as an unlikely Messiah (John 12:37) but actually condemned him for claiming to be the Son of God (Luke 22:71). Jesus' incarnation points to a critical challenge for humans faced with this God-choice about mediation: often we do not recognize God's mediated presence, even when it is the earthly face of the Son of God.

Eucharistic devotions take the mediated presence of God, particularly through the consecrated bread, very seriously. Similarly, a eucharistic spirituality resolutely embraces the mediated presence of God as an obligatory pathway toward our personal and collective holiness. Thus, a eucharistic spirituality, properly speaking, is an enfleshed, embodied, even creational spirituality.

While we will examine later the creational aspects of a eucharistic spirituality, it is first important to consider the mystery of humanity created in the image of God (Gen 1:27). This fundamental tenet of our faith was infinitely amplified through the mystery of the incarnation. The acknowledged center of that mystery is proclaimed in that dazzling statement from the prologue of the Gospel of John: "and the Word became flesh" (John 1:14). While Matthew and Luke's infancy narratives place this divine initiative in relatable and beloved narratives, John's broader theological perspective is the bedrock for this reflection. The mystery revealed in the Gospel of John is not simply that the Only Begotten was born, but that God was enfleshed, inextricably wed to humanity. This startling announcement escalated the previous biblical revelation that we were all created in the image of God. Now, this christological exclamation point affirms not only that we reflect or mirror something about God but that divinity has chosen to become one with humanity: all of humanity. Thus, incarnation is defined not only by the embodiment of God in Jesus but by a Christian belief in the embodiment of God in the whole of the human race.

One astonishing aspect of this mystery is that the incarnation did not conclude at the ascension, when Jesus departed this earthly realm. As theologian Anthony Kelly pointedly summarizes, "the incarnate Word has not been 'ex-carnated' by being raised and taken up into heaven."[5] Key here is the often-overlooked phrase in John's prologue that the enfleshed Word "dwelt among us." The English word *dwelt* might give the impression that this is a historical reporting of the limited number of years that the historical Jesus graced the earth with his presence. However, the actual Greek text behind our translations is much more ambiguous. It emphasizes the belief that God's enfleshment took place, but it does not define the duration of this "becoming flesh." Theologically, it is absolutely proper to reckon that God's "dwelling among us" in the flesh continues. Pope Francis confirms this approach when he notes,

> Indeed, the Gospel says that He came to dwell among us. He did not come to visit us, and then leave; He came to dwell with us, to stay with us. What, then, does He desire from us? He desires a great intimacy. He wants us to share with Him our joys and sufferings, desires and fears, hopes and sorrows, people and situations.[6]

Pope Francis unpacks this mystery further when he rejects the stance of being "starched Christians . . . who speak of theological matters as they sip their tea!" Instead, he urges us to be courageous, willing to "go in search of the people who are the very flesh of Christ." In essence, this is "the flesh of Christ, touching the flesh of Christ."[7] Specifically referencing what he calls "popular piety," Pope Francis further asserts in *The Joy of the Gospel* that genuine forms of popular religiosity are incarnate, born of the incarnation of faith in popular culture (91).

While this invitation is certainly daunting, the Eucharist and its devotions provide a clear path for pursuing such an enfleshed spirituality. At the heart of the eucharistic action is the basic human act of sharing food. As Monika Hellwig wisely noted, "The simple central human experience for the understanding of this action is hunger." She continues, "To be human is to be hungry. Not to be hungry is to be dead."[8] Jesus knew hunger so well that bread became a temptation (Matt 4:3). He also encountered the whole range of human hungers. Some of these were clearly spiritual, as exemplified in his encounter with the Samaritan woman. She was looking for physical water and Jesus promised to quench a deeper thirst (John 4:14). The Son of God did not simply offer spiritual remedies to folk. When questioned by John the Baptist's disciples about whether he was the true Messiah, he told them to go report back to John that the blind see, the lame walk, lepers are cleansed, the deaf hear, the dead are raised to life, and the Good News is preached. His was a consistently embodied mission and ministry. No text makes this clearer than the last judgment scene in Matthew (25:31-46). When the sheep are invited into the kingdom, it is not because they prayed for others in need or engaged in pious rituals. Rather, it is because they performed what we have come to know as the corporal works of mercy. Notably, the first of these is "I was hungry and you gave me food" (Matt 25:35).

A eucharistic spirituality is an embodied spirituality. It is one that recognizes the brutalizing hungers and needs of brothers and sisters—the lack of food, clean water, shelter from the elements, clothing, medicine, protection from exploitation and abuse—and then does something concrete to remedy these. Without such embodied enactment, eucharistic devotion can devolve into what Pope Francis has caricatured as the esoteric action of "starched Christians."

The Paschal: Drinking the Cup of Suffering

When previously considering the paschal nature of the Eucharist, we emphasized that the heart of sacrifice as revealed both in the Old and the New Testaments is not destruction of life or limb but rather a matter of the heart. As anticipated in the so called sacrifice of Abraham and as abundantly evidenced in Jesus' self-immolation at Golgotha, such a relinquishing of control—whether of one's own son (Isaac) or of one's own body (Jesus)—is neither the result of some punishment nor of some involuntary atonement. As the Jesuit theologian Robert Daly notes, this is not at its root a theology of negativity. Rather, central to authentic sacrifice is heart, is hope for a greater good, is a willingness to cede to others for a more wondrous future. In a word, it is about love.

One of the most obvious and consistent affirmations of a loving heart at the center of sacrifice is manifested in parents and grandparents, older siblings, and deeply committed relatives who empty themselves out for the sake of their dependents. How many times have you witnessed or experienced yourself the innumerable and sustained ways that family members have put your needs and those of others before their own? One friend opened my eyes to the touching stories of the thousands of health care workers from her part of the world who leave behind family and country—sometimes for many years—in order to earn higher wages that can be sent back to their families. She told me of one overseas health care worker from the Philippines whose parents had labored tirelessly to get her into a nursing program. When she graduated, it was her turn to take up the burden of supporting her younger siblings by emigrating to Chicago, where she acquired a well-paying nursing position. Living very frugally, the nurse admitted that sometimes she felt like an ATM, but her deep gratitude to her parents and love of her family kept her laboring on their behalf.

A rich biblical image for this loving stance is an often-overlooked part of the Johannine metaphor about vine and branches. During the long Last Supper discourse in John, Jesus speaks a consoling message about himself as the vine and us as the branches. If we remain in him, we will "bear much fruit" (John 15:5). While that verse easily comes to mind, we less often recall the previous verses about the pruning necessary to bring about such fruitfulness. Gardeners understand the importance of pruning, which requires trimming back aggressively growing branches and leaves so that the whole plant or vine will development. This is especially important for grape vines. If unpruned, they grow in wild and unruly ways, exploding with cascades of leaves that leave few nutrients for the fruit to grow. Thus, such pruning is not simply for the welfare of a single vine but to bring about an abundant harvest.

Jesus was a gifted mentor who often had to prune his own disciples so that the whole community of the beloved would flourish. Peter was pruned a number of times. The most notable occurrence takes place at the end of John's gospel, near the Sea of Galilee (John 21:15-17). Recalling Peter's triple denial, Jesus thrice asks Peter, "[D]o you love me . . .?" The Scriptures report that Peter is hurt by this repeated inquiry. Jesus' response, however, indicates that he is not simply interested in embarrassing Peter or taking him down a notch. After each of Peter's affirmations of love, Jesus missions him: "Feed my lambs. . . . Tend my sheep. . . . Feed my sheep." This formational moment for the prince of the apostles was not simply for his sake, but in service of God's reign.

Then follows a passage that receives very little attention: "[W]hen you were younger you dressed yourself and went where you wanted; but when you are old you will stretch out your hands, and someone else will dress you and lead you where you do not want to go" (John 21:18). This prophetic text not only indicates something of Peter's death but tells of the future path for every other disciple. We are all growing older. Some of us are becoming sicker; others are moving past our intellectual or physical prime. As our employability abates, our ability to play the game with the same vigor recedes, and our leadership skills start to atrophy, we become aware that nature itself is pruning us. We have little control over such decline: it is the future for all of us.

On the other hand, we do have control over how we respond to this natural ebbing of mind and body. While it is instinctive for us to hold on tightly to our position, our power, our prerogatives, Jesus models a different way. The Son of God allowed himself to be pruned in the most dramatic fashion at the end of his life: arrested, tried, stripped, scourged and crucified—all of it accepted by him out of love. Even in his ascension, he ceded his place on the earth so that disciples could take up his mission and be his new body in the world.

Deeply embedded in our eucharistic symbols are images of death and diminishment. Jesus definitively identifies himself as the "bread of life" and waxes eloquently about this new manna come down from heaven that bestows life on the world (John 6:32-35). At the same time, he metaphorically confirms that bread itself is marked with death. Unless a grain of wheat dies, it will not foster new life (John 12:24). As every baker knows, unless the wheat gives up its old life, the gift of bread itself is not possible. Even more than the bread, however, the cup of blessing so central to eucharistic feasting is saturated with images of diminishment and death. One of the most famous pruning scenes in the whole of the gospels occurs in the twentieth chapter of Matthew. The mother of the "sons of

Zebedee"—James and John—petitions Jesus to give her sons places of privilege in Jesus' kingdom. This request creates quite a stir among the other disciples, who are obviously miffed at this brazen request. In response, Jesus offers a critical litmus test: can they drink of the cup (Matt 20:22)? That is, are they willing to drink of Jesus' own Gethsemane cup (Matt 26:39) and offer their lives in service of Jesus' new kingdom?

Drinking of the consecrated wine brings us into the most intimate contact with the death of the Lord. This is the drinking of the "new covenant in [Jesus'] blood" (Luke 22:20). Rather than an isolated ritual moment, drinking from the cup is committing ourselves to a specific way of being in the world: of sacrificial living. While eucharistic devotions seldom focus on a consecrated cup of wine, the power of this central symbol must pervade all such devotions as it beckons us to sacrificial living.

In her astute reflection on eucharistic adoration, Joan Ridley considers the risk that occurs when the Eucharist is "exposed." She writes, "We may not be conscious of this reality, but the Lord takes a risk in being exposed. The risk is our rejection of his love, or worse—ridicule and disrespect. We who come before the Lord expose ourselves as well. We become both vulnerable and engaged with possibility."[9]

Like the Eucharist, authentic eucharistic devotion invites us into the very vulnerability of God in Christ, that our suffering as well as our inevitable diminishment might not turn us in on ourselves but graciously move us outward for the upbuilding of God's reign.

The Ecclesial: Befriending Neighbor and Stranger

Pondering the eucharistic mystery through an ecclesial framework could sound somewhat stuffy, even officious—especially if the first thing that comes to mind is church law or hierarchical structures. In shaping his followers, however, Jesus adopted a highly relational, even intimate approach that reveals hospitality and deep care at the heart of the church he birthed on the cross. This is especially highlighted in his Last Supper discourse recorded in the Gospel of John:

> This is my commandment, that you love one another as I have loved you. No one has greater love than this, to lay down one's life for one's friends. You are my friends if you do what I command you. I do not call you servants any longer, because the servant does not know what the master is doing; but I have called you friends, because I have made known to you everything that I have heard from my Father. (John 15:12-15)

This is a text we have heard often, and because of its repetition, it might sound quite tame to us. However, Scripture scholar Gerhard Lohfink exposes the revolutionary approach Jesus adopts here with his followers by comparing Jesus to other rabbis of the time. According to Lohfink, the very fact that Jesus "called" disciples was unheard of. Rabbinic students of the day sought out their own teachers. One of the reasons for this freedom of choice is that after choosing a rabbi, the disciple literally became the rabbi's servant. "This 'serving' means that the student performs for the teacher all of the services that would otherwise be done by a servant or a slave. He washes the rabbi's feet, serves at and clears the table, cleans the house and the courtyard, goes to the market and purchases necessities."[10] In this context, Jesus completely upends expectations of what it means to be a disciple for his inner circle and, by extension, to every subsequent follower. We are not to lord it over one another but to serve in the example of this humble messiah (Matt 20:25-28). Ecclesial living and the discipleship that flows from it presumes extending Jesus' friendship to each other and the world.

Not surprisingly, the language of friendship is often associated with eucharistic devotions. In his 1947 encyclical on the liturgy, *Mediator Dei*,[11] Pope Pius XII recognized that when we adore Christ in the Eucharist, not only do we pray for favors but the church "professes her gratitude to him and she enjoys the intimacy of his friendship" (131). The *Directory on Popular Piety and the Liturgy* echoes this teaching when it describes Eucharist this way: "Abiding with Christ the Lord, [the faithful] enjoy his intimate friendship and pour out their hearts before him for themselves and for those dear to them and they pray for the peace and salvation of the world" (164).

Another useful framework, so very rich in exposing the more challenging side of friendship, is that of encounter. Already in the mid-twentieth century, the respected Belgian theologian and Vatican II consultant Edward Schillebeeckx (d. 2009) deployed this language in his attempts to render sacramental theology less abstract and more personal. His most accessible exploration of this concept appeared in his 1959 classic work, soon translated from Dutch into English as *Christ, The Sacrament of the Encounter with God*.[12] The language of encounter was eagerly and widely embraced in much theological and pastoral discourse. The *Catechism of the Catholic Church* adopts it when discussing the sacraments, noting that each liturgical action—especially the Eucharist and other sacraments—"is an encounter between Christ and the Church" (1097).

Few magisterial documents embrace the dynamics of encounter more than Pope Francis's *The Joy of the Gospel*. Not only does the word *encounter* appear dozens of times in that exhortation—starting with its opening sentence—but more importantly, the theme of encounter is central to the pope's understanding of discipleship and evangelization. Besides inviting all Christians "to a renewed personal encounter with Jesus Christ" (3) that "blossoms into . . . friendship" (8), Francis repeatedly defines our shared Christian vocation as missionary disciples by our willingness to encounter others. For example, he writes:

> Many try to escape from others and take refuge in the comfort of their privacy or in a small circle of close friends, renouncing the realism of the social aspect of the Gospel. For just as some people want a purely spiritual Christ, without flesh and without the cross, they also want their interpersonal relationships provided by sophisticated equipment, by screens and systems which can be turned on and off on command. Meanwhile, the Gospel tells us constantly to run the risk of a face-to-face encounter with others, with their physical presence which challenges us, with their pain and their pleas, with their joy which infects us in our close and continuous interaction. (88)

Pope Francis gives particular attention to popular piety and devotions, as a true expression of the "spontaneous missionary activity of the people of God" (122), and thus a privileged place where this drive toward encounter is nourished.

A revered gospel story that underscores both the challenge and promise of encounter is Luke's post-resurrection saga of the two disciples on the road to Emmaus (24:13-35). This surprising tale of rejections and reversals opens with the duo traveling northwest on a trail that places Jerusalem clearly at their backs. This geography of the terrain symbolizes a spiritual geography at play here: these two are leaving ministry behind and setting out on a new life path. Then they unexpectedly meet the stranger. Of course, when we hear this passage we know that the interloper is Jesus. In order to grasp something of the dynamism of the narrative, however, it is necessary to suspend momentarily that knowledge. The recently resigned disciples do not know it is the Lord. It is notable that in the story the stranger makes the first move, asking about the lively discussion that was apparently consuming them on their journey. The downcast pair promptly share their tale of disappointment, even grief. While their shared telling does have a glimmer of hope in the tale of an empty tomb, apparently it was insufficiently convincing to keep the two of them in Jerusalem. Then the tables turn as the stranger convincingly reinterprets the messianic prophecies so well known to them. This chance meeting has become so enlightening that now it is their turn to take the initiative, pressing the Lord to share a meal. His signature act of God-blessing and bread-breaking that so marked his public ministry is the final trigger as the Risen One vanishes from their sight. While on the one hand, the literary climax of the tale occurs when the two announce back in Jerusalem how they recognized the Lord in the breaking of the bread, the vocational climax occurred previously when the pair changed course and turned southeast toward that ancient Jewish capital. In so doing, they re-embraced their discipleship and symbolically opened themselves to their own martyrdom by returning to the place of Jesus' recent passion and death.

Pope Francis writes in *The Joy of the Gospel* that "whenever we encounter another person in love, we learn something new about God" (272). Eucharistic adoration, like other devotions to the Blessed Sacrament, draws us into a decidedly consequential encounter with Jesus Christ. A divine friendship is truly extended to us in these rituals, as it is in the eucharistic liturgy that anchors such devotions. This encounter, however, does not beckon us to remain only in solitude with the Lord. Rather it substantially feeds us for those risky face-to-face encounters that mark our own missionary discipleship.

The Missiological: Humbled by God's Spirit

In the previous chapter, when considering theologies drawn from eucharistic practice and belief, we highlighted an important evolution that had developed among missiologists in the twentieth century. That evolution concerned a fresh perception not only for considering specific missionary endeavors but, more importantly, for understanding the church as missionary at its core. The phrase we drew upon to summarize this change is *missio Dei*, or the "mission of God," which underscores that mission is not so much an activity of the church as much as it is an attribute of the Lord of all Creation.

When we ponder the parallel spirituality that springs from this theological advancement, another potent phrase comes to mind: *mission in reverse*. This is a concept that developed among my colleagues at Catholic Theological Union in Chicago in the 1980s. Claude-Marie Barbour, herself once a missionary in South Africa, defined this reversal as an approach which teaches "that the minister can and should learn from the people ministered to—including, and perhaps especially, from the poor and marginalized people."[13] There are powerful and unsettling insights that flow from this revisioning of ministry. One of them is a recognition that every act of evangelization is a mutual dialogue rather than a one-way delivery system from the missionary to the apparently unenlightened or un-saved. Another piece of wisdom that amplifies this gift of mutuality concerns the role of the Holy Spirit.

Stephen Bevans is a helpful guide here. He notes that most Christian theologies imagine the place of the Holy Spirit through frameworks provided by the Gospel of John. The divine progression developed from this Johannine lens has God sending Jesus and Jesus, in turn, sending the Spirit (e.g., John 16:5-7). Recently, however, a complementary theological position has emerged that gives a different priority to the Holy Spirit. In this schema, God first sends the Spirit, who prepared the way for the Son to complete God's saving work.[14] There are an abundance of texts from the Old and New Testaments that support this position. For example, as Bevans recounts, it is God's Spirit who hovers over the waters at Creation (Gen 1:2), who endows prophets with authority to speak God's word (Mic 3:8), who calls Israel back from unfaithfulness (Hos 10:12), who restores life (Ezek 37:1-14), and who ultimately transforms hearts of stone (Ezek 36:25-28). In the New Testament, it is by the power of the Spirit that Mary conceives the Only Begotten (Luke 1:35), it is God's Spirit that was poured out on Jesus in his baptism (Matt 3:16), who then leads him into the wilderness (Matt 4:1), and who ultimately sets the agenda for Jesus' ministry (Luke 4:18-19).

When expounding his vision of evangelization in *The Joy of the Gospel*, Pope Francis gives ample attention to the Holy Spirit. Affirming that Jesus himself was animated by the Holy Spirit (5), the pope teaches that it is the power of God's Spirit that leads us into "every activity of evangelization" (12) and that every ministry is "animated by the fire of the Spirit" (14). He also confirms that popular piety and its practices manifest the gratuitous initiative of the Holy Spirit (125). Maybe even more surprisingly, the pope also affirms that one experiences the Holy Spirit working in the world apart from the Catholic Church. When speaking about our Orthodox sisters and brothers, for example, the pope asserts that "if we really believe in the abundantly free working of the Holy Spirit, we can learn so much from one another. . . . reaping what the Spirit has sown in them, which is also meant to be a gift for us" (246). Beyond Orthodox Christianity, he acknowledges that "the Holy Spirit is at work in everyone" (178). He specifically acknowledges non-Christians as people who "can be channels which the Holy Spirit raises up" continuing: "The same Spirit everywhere brings forth various forms of practical wisdom which help people to bear suffering and to live in greater peace and harmony" (254). A eucharistic spirituality worthy of missionary disciples can neither corral God's Spirit nor dissuade Divine Wisdom from blowing where it will. Beyond what it cannot do, such a spirituality must cultivate virtues of both humility and generosity.

For some, humility may loom as the default position of the powerless that allows or even welcomes the demeaning of our human dignity. Christian revelation, however, offers a different interpretive lens. The firstborn of all creation not only spoke of the blessedness of the humble (Matt 5:5) but also self-identified as meek and humble of heart (Matt 11:29). More astonishing, his lived ministry surpassed this rhetoric. Here is the very incarnation of God who at birth was laid in a feeding trough for animals (Luke 2:7), had no place to lay his head (Matt 8:20), washed the feet of his disciples (John 13:5ff), allowed himself to be arrested, mocked, stripped, was sentenced like a common criminal, then led like a lamb to slaughter (Isa 53:7), and ultimately even had to be buried in a borrowed tomb (Luke 23:53). As summarized by St. Paul in his letter to the Philippians, Jesus is one who did not exploit his equality with God, but assumed the nature of a servant, humbling himself even to death on a cross (Phil 2:6-7). On the other hand, what could we expect from the son of a woman who, early in her pregnancy, celebrated her lowliness as a gift from the Most High (Luke 1:48)?

St. Francis of Assisi embraced this wondrous virtue as the center of his own spirituality and the hallmark of those who would follow Christ with him. In a particular way, Francis praises what he calls the "sublime humility" of God as revealed in the Eucharist. In his letter to the whole Franciscan Order, he writes:

> O sublime humility!
> O humble sublimity!
> The Lord of the universe,
> God and the Son of God,
> So humbles himself
> That for our salvation
> He hides himself
> Under an ordinary piece of Bread!
> Brothers, look at the humility of God
> And pour out your hearts before him.

Humble yourselves
That you may be exalted by him!
Hold back nothing of yourselves for yourselves,
That he Who gives Himself totally to you
May receive you totally![15]

Eucharistic worship and the devotions that flow from it are an invitation to encounter the very humility of God in Christ. Immersed in this divine meekness, we are led in the Spirit to the same openness that marked the earthly ministry of Jesus. His generous hospitality welcomed the high born and children, the virtuous and reviled, those at the center of power and those on the margins, the healthy and the leprous. Sometimes those encounters surprised him, as when an unknown woman secretly touched his cloak in the hope of being healed (Luke 8:44). On other occasions, such chance meetings changed him, as did that with the Syrophoenician woman who effectively challenged Jesus to heal her daughter (Mark 7:24-30). This sacred openness and deep humility is so central to God's incarnation in Christ that it is eternally symbolized in the crucifixion: Jesus nailed to the cross in a timeless stance of hospitality with arms stretched wide in a holy gesture of unlimited welcome.

The Spirit of God is yet afoot in our world, sown in the hearts of people of good will in every nation, regardless of race or language, across the range of human gifts and abilities. A spirituality aligned to God's mission and forged in the eucharistic humility of God in Christ compels our receptivity to this unleashing of divine wisdom wherever it arises. Pope Francis consistently prods us into such openness, even deeming those who are not part of any religious tradition "precious allies" in the defense of human dignity and the task of peace-building (*The Joy of the Gospel*, 257). When we practice this truly catholic largesse, the promise of mission in reverse is increasingly realized, as we are changed, enriched, and even graced by unexpected emissaries of God's Spirit.

The Ecological:
Living a Harmonious Ethic

In 1983 Cardinal Joseph Bernardin (d. 1996) delivered a prophetic speech at Fordham University in New York on the theme of a "consistent ethic of life." At the time, the cardinal was the chair of the US bishops' pro-life committee. His goal was to promote reverence for all aspects of life and oppose every threat to life from abortion to capital punishment. Surprising to some, this "seamless garment" approach also addressed issues of hunger and homelessness as well as the quality of life for immigrants and unemployed workers.[16] As he developed this concept over the years, Cardinal Bernardin expanded and clarified this approach, which he championed with increasing vigor. As he explained in another university lecture, the main goal was to have a systematic vision of life in which the church and its members—across a wide spectrum of opinions and beliefs—together cultivate a conscious and explicit connection across these challenging issues.[17] This language of consistency and seamlessness is effective for imagining a eucharistic spirituality that ranges across the multiple facets that we have explored in these pages. It is also particularly useful when we envision this spirituality from an ecological perspective.

Ecospirituality is often initially understood as concerned primarily with how human beings treat or mistreat the natural world. For Christians, the ethics behind such a stance are found in the Scriptures and other teachings from our tradition that instruct us about the goodness of creation and its intrinsic value for giving God glory. We rehearsed some of these sources in the last chapter. An initial response to these revelations and theologies is a recognition that human beings have been a major force in the destruction of our environment. In a joint statement, Ecumenical Patriarch Bartholomew (b. 1940) and Pope St. John Paul II recognized that such destructiveness is appropriately categorized as an ecological sin.[18] It may be shocking to learn that a good number of environmentalists have actually linked exploitation of nature with Judeo-Christian narratives, particularly those that seem to assert the priority of humans over creation. A prime example they lift up in this challenge is the Genesis text in which God gives human beings dominion over all the earth (Gen 1:26).

The lived response to such human exploitation is manifest in a wide variety of individual and collective actions, from recycling and the banning of plastic bags, to growing trends in industry to move away from fossil fuels, to government policies to reduce deforestation. One notable development in response to the continued degradation of creation is the emergence of a "reconciliation ecology." This has been described as "the science of inventing, establishing, and maintaining new habitats to conserve species diversity in places where people live, work, or play."[19] As David Warners and his colleagues further explain, this approach turns the focus back onto humanity and asks, "How can we reconfigure our own existence so that it is more a blessing than a curse to the broader landscape within which we reside?"[20]

This broadening environmental perspective finds both resonance and expansion in Pope Francis's understanding of ecology. Invoking the language of "the seamless garment" in reference to God's creation, the pope promotes a wide-angle approach to what he calls an "integral ecology" in his encyclical *Laudato Si'*. Grounded in the belief that everything is interconnected (70), Pope Francis asserts our mutuality with nature, which is not something separate from us since "[w]e are part of nature" (139). This integrated view allows him to understand that environmental crises and social crises are not separate but rather "one complex crisis which is both social and environmental" (139). Consequently, we cannot address issues of climate change or the pollution of our oceans apart from the challenges of unemployment, poverty, or restoring dignity to the excluded. Thus, the pope expends considerable energy in *Laudato Si'* addressing the quality of human life and the breakdown of society. In a breathtaking summary of this deeply integrated view of ecology, Pope Francis writes:

> A sense of deep communion with the rest of nature cannot be real if our hearts lack tenderness, compassion and concern for our fellow human beings. It is clearly inconsistent to combat trafficking in endangered species while remaining completely indifferent to human trafficking, unconcerned about the poor, or undertaking to destroy another human being deemed unwanted. . . . Everything is connected. (91)

Spirituality is not simply about personal piety and crafting our individual path to salvation. Rather, as Pope Francis has clarified, a Christian spirituality is a vision of an integrated and ethical view of life. In describing some of the characteristics of such a spirituality he writes:

> Christian spirituality proposes a growth marked by moderation and the capacity to be happy with little. It is a return to that simplicity which allows us to stop and appreciate the small things, to be grateful for the opportunities which life affords us, to be spiritually detached from what we possess, and not to succumb to sadness for what we lack. This implies avoiding the dynamic of dominion and the mere accumulation of pleasures. (222)

This summary harmonizes well with the Jesus revealed in the gospels. The utter simplicity of the Lord's life was startling, without even a place for the Son of God to "lay his head" (Luke 9:58). He embodied the opposite of dominion in his servant approach to ministry and his consistent teaching in word and deed that his followers must embody the same. Jesus was detached from the world and its possessions, even unto death. At the same time, Jesus wove his own humility seamlessly into his ethical approach to all life and human dignity. No outcast, no marginalized, no insignificant individual in the eyes of the world was insignificant to him. Jesus was the very incarnation of an integral ecology, raising up the dignity of the poor and infusing humble fruits of the earth (bread and a cup of wine) with his own divine presence.

Engaging in eucharistic devotions, with their traditional focus on these humble elements, draws us into a similar seamlessness of adoration and ethics. We cannot honor consecrated bread and wine without caring for the earth that nurtured the elements of wheat and grapes eventually transformed by human hands. We cannot worship foodstuffs transformed into the body of Christ without a profound commitment to address the rampant food insecurity that threatens so much of the world's population. The integrity of this vision is well summarized by Pope Francis in this prayer for our earth and all of its inhabitants:

> All-powerful God, you are present in the whole universe
> and in the smallest of your creatures.
> You embrace with your tenderness all that exists.
> Pour out upon us the power of your love,
> that we may protect life and beauty.
> Fill us with peace, that we may live
> as brothers and sisters, harming no one.
> O God of the poor,
> help us to rescue the abandoned and forgotten of this earth,
> so precious in your eyes.
> Bring healing to our lives,
> that we may protect the world and not prey on it,
> that we may sow beauty, not pollution and destruction.
> Touch the hearts
> of those who look only for gain
> at the expense of the poor and the earth.
> Teach us to discover the worth of each thing,
> to be filled with awe and contemplation,
> to recognize that we are profoundly united

with every creature
as we journey towards your infinite light.
We thank you for being with us each day.
Encourage us, we pray, in our struggle
for justice, love and peace. (*Laudato Si'* 246)

Summary

The invitation to receive Christ's presence under the ap-
pearances of a morsel of bread and a cup of wine is at once the
simplest of actions and the most serious of commitments. Because of the ease with which so many Roman Catholics can
participate in this sacrament, sometimes the profound implications of our eucharistic reception can be underappreciated or
even overlooked. As St. Paul makes so clear in his writings to
the church in Corinth (1 Cor 11–12), however, we receive the
bread of life and the cup of salvation with the weighty purpose
of becoming Christ's body poured out in service to each other
and the world. Living that commitment, however modestly
or quietly, is living a distinctive eucharistic spirituality. Since
eucharistic adoration and its allied practices and devotions are
graced prolongations of the eucharistic mystery in time and
space, they are by extension also unique rehearsals of a spirituality deeply rooted in the Eucharist and the baptismal vows
that opened the way for our participation in this sacred communion. We pray that we might increasingly engage in these
devotions with hearts wide open, allowing us to be immersed
in an inestimable gift that beckons us to be gifts to others.

Chapter Four

Principles and Guidelines
for Pastoral Practice

Introduction

In the opening lines of the *Constitution on the Sacred Liturgy* (*CSL*), the bishops of the Second Vatican Council set out in unambiguous language precisely why they undertook the important work of liturgical reform. Among the many possible aims of such an undertaking, their first expressed purpose was "to impart an ever-increasing vigor to the Christian lives of the faithful" (1). As noted early on in this volume, the respected church historian Massimo Faggioli would further contend that the agenda of the liturgical constitution actually served as a roadmap for the unfolding of the remainder of Vatican II and its fifteen major documents that would be promulgated in the ensuing years. In a similar way, many would agree that a primary purpose not only of this first document of the council but the council itself was to impart an ever-increasing vigor to the Christian lives of the faithful. Thus, while the *Constitution on the Sacred Liturgy*—like the other council documents— offered theological clarifications, invoked biblical foundations, and provided essential directives for the reform, the main reason for this undertaking was for the sake of Christian living.

Similarly, we have explored historical and biblical precedents for eucharistic adoration and devotion as well as articulated theological principles for these in the first two chapters of this book. Such preparatory work was undertaken for the purpose of nourishing a well-lived eucharistic faith among the baptized. In many ways, therefore, the previous chapter on spirituality lies at the heart of this venture. At the same time, however, we recall that it is the liturgy—rather than the talking or writing about worship—that is the fount and summit of the church's life (*CSL* 10). Roman Catholic worship is an event. While it often utilizes books, it is not a book. While it typically employs ritual objects, it is not an object. While it occupies spaces and has ministers donning vestments and allows for a variety of different instruments, liturgy is none of these things. Rather, our worship is full-bodied enactment rooted in the saving work of Christ. Thus, as we noted early on in this volume, the *Constitution on the Sacred Liturgy* declares a truth worth repeating:

> [E]very liturgical celebration, because it is an action of Christ the priest and of his body, which is the church, is a preeminently sacred action. No other action of the church equals its effectiveness by the same title nor to the same degree. (7)

Because the church's official liturgy and the devotions that flow from it are by their very nature redemptive events, in the final analysis it is the actual doing of the worship that requires our ultimate and thoughtful attention here. In service of Vatican II's intent to reform worship so that it imparts an ever-increasing vigor to the Christian lives of the faithful, it is critical that pastoral agents and the faithful they serve have credible yet accessible principles and guidelines for shaping such worship. As the council fathers noted, such norms go beyond careful attention to the rubrics and laws that render our worship both valid and licit (*CSL* 11). While it is absolutely essentially to attend to such rubrics and directives, it is also insufficient simply to enact the church's rites with juridical accuracy. That is why the constitution speaks about the need for pastors to demonstrate energy, to be imbued with the spirit of the liturgy (11), to demonstrate diligence and patience (19), and to lead by example. Even more telling, one of the words that appears with striking consistently throughout the English translation of that pivotal document is *care*. One can rightfully conclude from this language that one should not only "care" for the liturgy, but that the liturgy itself be an act of pastoral care.

Official Pastoral Guidelines

The contribution of thoughtful principles and guidelines in crafting careful and "caring" worship is particularly important when it comes to devotions. This contention is rooted in the reality that many such pious acts often emerge out of local customs, are lay led, and are infrequently included in the church's official books. Consequently, many devotions lack any explicitly sanctioned directives or protocols.

There are some important pastoral instructions in the 1973 ritual Holy Communion and Worship of the Eucharist outside Mass. Admittedly, this official ritual is not directly concerned with "devotion" but rather addresses multiple official Roman Catholic liturgies outlined in that document, such as administering Communion outside of Mass and exposition of the Holy Eucharist. By extension, however, the pastoral guidance offered for these key eucharistic rituals also provides insight into the shaping of eucharistic devotions. Some of the more relevant directives found in this 1973 ritual include:

- "[t]he primary and original reason for reservation of the eucharist outside Mass is the administration of viaticum" (5),

- "[t]he union with Christ, to which the sacrament is directed, should be extended to the whole of Christian life" (25),

- being "[n]ourished by God's word" leads "to grateful and fruitful participation" in the Eucharist (26),

- the liturgical seasons should be taken into account when arranging eucharistic devotions (79),

- eucharistic devotions are directed toward "both sacramental and spiritual communion" (80),

- the faithful engaging in such devotions should be concerned with good deeds (81),

- exposition of the Blessed Sacrament should occur only if there are suitable numbers of the faithful (83, 86),

- a homily or exhortation that unfolds the eucharistic mystery is helpful (95), and

- eucharistic processions are a form of "public witness" and "devotion" (101).

Building on the pastoral instincts of this important reformed rite, as well as drawing upon other magisterial and theological resources, the *Directory on Popular Piety and the Liturgy* offers further intelligent and authoritative counsel on the broader field of popular piety. Some of its basic principles include:

- recognizing the primacy of the church's official liturgy over any other form of prayer (11),

- the gospel as the measure for all expressions of Christian piety (12),

- the importance of Scripture (12),

- the need for "a correct evaluation and renewal of pious exercises and devotional practices" in the spirit of Vatican II (12),

- the importance of linking public gestures with a "commitment to live the Christian life" (15), and

- the conservation of traditional music, yet with openness to the possibility of their revision or new compositions (17).

When it comes to eucharistic devotions, that directory articulates a few more specific guidelines, including:

- "all forms of Eucharistic devotion must have an intrinsic reference" to the Mass (161),

- in eucharistic adoration "the faithful should be encouraged to read the Scriptures" (165),

- "suitable hymns and canticles based on those of the Liturgy of the Hours and the liturgical seasons could also be encouraged" (165),

- "silent prayer and reflection" have an important role (165),

- "the faithful should be encouraged not to do other devotional exercises during exposition of the Blessed Sacrament" (165), with the exception that:

- the rosary, with its "Christological orientation, . . . can always be of assistance" (165).

Finally, in his 2013 exhortation, *The Joy of the Gospel*, Pope Francis gives special attention to what he calls "popular piety" (69), asserting that its many and varied expressions have much to teach us (127). As in other documents, much of what Francis teaches is more theological and spiritual. At the same time, a few key pastoral directives about popular piety and their devotions stand out in his work. Four seem particularly important:

- inculturation is a central characteristic of popular religiosity (127),

- forms of "popular spirituality" are "incarnated in the culture of the lowly" and thus accessible to all (125),

- popular piety and its practices are important tools for evangelization (123), and

- genuine forms of popular religiosity are at their core relational and should foster relationships with God, the saints, and each other (91).

A Pastoral-Liturgical Synthesis

These multiple strands of pastoral and devotional guidelines are a wellspring of wisdom for those of us engaged in the shaping and performing of eucharistic adoration and devotions. At the same time, however, the way these guidelines emerge in these various documents does not always provide a sense of coherence or any clear indication of their sequencing or priority. Furthermore, there appear to be some implicit presuppositions in these communications that may not always be apparent at first reading. Without presuming to replace such valued counsel, therefore, it yet seems useful to synthesize them in a way that might be more pastorally comprehensible and digestible. Thus, I offer the following five frameworks to aid the important and often neglected ministry of shaping and leading eucharistic adoration and its allied devotions.

Planning and Preparation: Individual authors, local parishes, and sprawling Roman Catholic dioceses are just some of the voices that speak with varying degrees of authority about liturgical planning. This has resulted in countless books, articles, diocesan and parochial guidelines, and all of those individual planning sheets for weddings, funerals, and especially Sunday worship. Interestingly enough, few official Roman Catholic liturgical documents speak explicitly about the critical pastoral task of planning worship. For example, it is not a topic directly addressed in the *Constitution on the Sacred Liturgy.*

The *General Instruction of the Roman Missal* does note that the entire eucharistic liturgy is to be "arranged in such a way that it leads to a conscious, active, and full participation of the faithful, namely in body and in mind" (18). It also advises that at least in cathedrals as well as in larger churches there should be some "competent minister . . . to see to the appropriate arrangement of sacred actions" (106). Maybe most important are the directives in chapter VII, on "The Choice of the Mass and Its Parts." The very nature of this chapter presumes that serious preparation is essential. Some of this is directed to the priest-presider, who "in arranging the celebration of Mass, . . . should be attentive rather to the common spiritual good of the People of God than to his own inclinations" (352). It concludes in that same paragraph that "harmonious ordering and carrying out of the rites will greatly help in disposing the faithful for participation in the Eucharist" (352).

One of the characteristics of many devotions is their rootedness in respected traditions and their tendency to repeat deeply ingrained prayer practices. While Benediction of the Blessed Sacrament is technically not a devotion but an official liturgy, this penchant for repetition is well illustrated in the way Benediction is celebrated in many places today. Although they are not mentioned as a part of the official Rite of Eucharistic Exposition and Benediction, the Divine Praises as well as the hymn "Holy God, We Praise Thy Name" are widely regarded as invariable elements of the rite. They certainly were in the 1950s, when I was an altar server for such events. Yet the rites revised after Vatican II and various directives noted above indicate that there are more significant components that may be included in these rites, such as the use of Scripture and preaching. Unfortunately, these suggestions are regularly neglected.

Not to plan is to plan poorly. While respecting the traditions of pious exercises and devotional practices, "the liturgical renewal willed by the Second Vatican Council must also inspire a correct evaluation and renewal of these" (*Directory on Popular Piety and the Liturgy*, 17). In this spirit, regular planning and thoughtful preparation needs to include processes for evaluation and renewal. Such procedures can only infuse new vibrancy into these much-beloved rites. Such planning is also an important tool for achieving some level of cultural adaptation that both the *Constitution on the Sacred Liturgy* (37–40) and the *Directory on Popular Piety and the Liturgy* (91–92) acknowledge as valuable. While eucharistic devotional practices should be recognizable across contexts and cultures, they need not look the same in every context and culture.

Many forms of eucharistic devotion and adoration, such as visits to the Blessed Sacrament, are quite personal—even somewhat individualistic—and might seem to fall outside any need or even possibility for planning, evaluation, or renewal. On the other hand, properly preparing an environment for eucharistic adoration or visits to the Blessed Sacrament according to the church's general guidelines for devotions can inevitably enhance those experiences. For example, prayer cards with texts from the Bread of Life discourse in John 6 or changes in the environment that echo the unfolding of the various liturgical seasons can encourage prayer more precisely aligned with the Sunday Eucharist. Such preparatory practices respect the repeated injunction that eucharistic devotions should always be drawn from and lead people back to the church's official eucharistic liturgy. Engaging in planning and evaluation also helps safeguard against pious practices that veer away from the underlying "communitarian and ecclesial aspects of prayer" (*Directory on Popular Piety and the Liturgy*, 35).

Scripture: One of the great achievements of Vatican II was its embrace of the essential, even sacramental role of God's Word in worship and Christian life. Thus, the *Constitution on the Sacred Liturgy* proclaims that Christ is "present in his word since it is he himself who speaks when the holy scriptures are read in Church" (7). That theological assertion allows the council fathers to assert that "sacred scripture is of the greatest importance in the celebration of the liturgy" (*CSL* 24). Furthermore, the *Dogmatic Constitution on Divine Revelation* magisterially teaches that, together with sacred tradition, Scripture is the "supreme rule of . . . faith" (21). In addition, that document confirms that, along with sacred tradition, Scripture is the primary and perpetual foundation of theology (24). In that spirit, the documents of Vatican II are heavily accented with biblical references, rooting the reforms deeply in God's Word.

Given this scriptural turn—an admitted gift from our sister churches who have long championed the importance of God's Word in theology and worship—it is not surprising that revised rites for eucharistic liturgies and devotion place such emphasis on biblical texts. Central is the liturgical constitution's directive that "the treasures of the bible are to be opened up more lavishly so that a richer fare may be provided for the faithful at the table of God's word" (*CSL* 51). An important subtext of this directive that echoes through the multiple directives about eucharistic adoration and devotion cited above is that these scriptural treasures should also enrich, enhance, and pervade practices of popular piety in general and eucharistic devotion in particular.

When discussing the practice of adoration, the Rite of Eucharistic Exposition and Benediction instructs "there should be readings from scripture" (95). This language is echoed in the *Directory on Popular Piety and the Liturgy*, which notes, "The faithful should be encouraged to read the Scriptures during these periods of [eucharistic] adoration, since they afford an unrivalled source of prayer" (165). The language here is important. This official rite of the church and a magisterial directory are not suggesting that some readings might be a nice addition, or that if it is convenient some biblical passage might be proclaimed. Rather, the language of "should" underscores the complementary and integral role Scripture plays in the church's eucharistic worship. The *Constitution on the Sacred Liturgy* teaches that the faithful are to be nourished at the "table of the Lord's Body" (48). Significantly, this magisterial teaching also employs that same metaphor when it speaks about the role of Scripture, noting that people are also to be richly nourished "at the table of God's word" (51). These "two tables" of divine revelation are inseparable in the celebration of the Mass. By consequence, if eucharistic devotions not only should "accord" with the sacred liturgy but also in some way be "derived from it and lead the people to it" (13) then the dynamic interaction of these dual tables of word and sacrament needs to be reflected in them as well. As the *Directory on Popular Piety and the Liturgy* instructs, "popular piety should be permeated by a biblical spirit, since it is impossible to image a Christian prayer without direct or indirect reference to Sacred Scripture" (12).

There are multiple ways that such scriptural resonance can be incorporated into public and private eucharistic adoration and devotions. One seldom-explored possibility is the suggestion from the Rite of Eucharistic Exposition and Benediction to incorporate parts of the Liturgy of the Hours into adoration (96). This official prayer of the church is deeply grounded in Scripture, especially the psalms. During extended periods of exposition, it is quite appropriate to pray this liturgy, which "extends the praise and thanksgiving offered to God in the eucharistic celebration to the several hours of the day" (96). More simply, appropriate excerpts from the Divine Office could be made available in places of adoration. Often there are booklets or other prayer aids available in such places. Why not provide selections from the church's official prayer as well? The opening versicle from the hours, "God, come to my assistance. Lord, make haste to help me" (Ps 69:2), is a splendid way to begin any visit to the Blessed Sacrament. Classic morning prayer in the ancient celebration of this ecclesial prayer began with Psalm 63. It is also frequently employed as a responsorial psalm during Mass. The responsorial form of this psalm, found in the Lectionary (for example, at no. 96C), easily lends itself to public or private recitation before the Blessed Sacrament:

Response: My soul is thirsting for you, O Lord my God.

O God, you are my God whom I seek;
   for you my flesh pines and my soul thirsts
   like the earth, parched, lifeless and without water.
   (Response)

Thus have I gazed toward you in the sanctuary
   to see your power and your glory,
for your kindness is a greater good than life;
   my lips shall glorify you. (Response)

Thus will I bless you while I live;
   lifting up my hands, I will call upon your name.
As with the riches of a banquet shall my soul be satisfied,
   and with exultant lips my mouth shall praise you.
   (Response)

You are my help,
   and in the shadow of your wings I shout for joy.
My soul clings fast to you;
   your right hand upholds me. (Response)

Excerpts from Jesus' Last Supper discourse in the Gospel of John are also rich scriptural prompts for prayer and contemplation. Jesus' instruction that he is the way, the truth, and the life (John 14:6), his discourse on the vine and branches (John 15:1ff), and particularly his instruction to "abide in [his] love" (John 15:9) are apt prayer cues before the Blessed Sacrament. Providing these or similar scriptural resources is a respectful way in which pastors and other pastoral agents can carry out the presumed planning that the *General Instruction of the Roman Missal* notes is of such great "help in disposing the faithful for participation in the Eucharist" (352).

Liturgical Year: There are few aspects of public worship as easily recognized and appreciated by believers of every age as the shifting cycles of the liturgical seasons. Vestments change from green to purple to white as we travel from Ordinary Time through Lent to Easter. Sanctuary appointments evolve from simple plant or flower arrangements to elaborate nativity sets that are often flanked by flocked fir trees or other Christmas greenery in the Northern Hemisphere as we prepare to celebrate the incarnational feast. Then there are the shifts in the sonic environment. Even blindfolded, most Roman Catholics could discern the onset of a new liturgical season because of the music. We only sing "O Come, O Come Emmanuel" or "Silent Night" or "Jesus Christ Is Risen Today" in particular seasons. The shifting repertoire, even in parishes with very modest music programs, is a reliable cue for calculating our festal location through the church year.

The seasons of the church year are ancient strategies that evolved as aids for prayerfully engaging those central mysteries revealed in the life of Christ. The breadth of this engagement is recognized by the *Constitution on the Sacred Liturgy*, which teaches us that by recalling the mysteries of our redemption, the liturgical year "opens up to the faithful the riches of the Lord's powers and merits, so that these are in some way made present at all times; the faithful lay hold of them and are filled with saving grace" (102).

The impact of the various seasons of the liturgical year on the church's official liturgy, especially on the celebration of the Eucharist, is enormous. Most obvious in this regard are the proper orations and prefaces in Advent, Christmas, Lent, and Easter that are especially calibrated to proclaim central aspects of the mystery of God in Christ. These prayer forms tune the hearts of the faithful to key revelations from our salvation history in order to deepen our commitment to live fully these mysteries in our own lives. A good example of such a prayer is the collect for the Mass for the First Sunday of Advent:

Grant your faithful, we pray, almighty God,
the resolve to run forth to meet your Christ
with righteous deeds at his coming,
so that, gathered at his right hand,
they may be worthy to possess the heavenly Kingdom.
Through our Lord Jesus Christ, your Son,
who lives and reigns with you in the unity of the Holy Spirit,
one God, for ever and ever.

In a concise and accessible way, this prayer announces one of Advent's most central themes: Christ's coming at the end of time. It does so, however, by requesting the grace to live a righteous life as the appropriate preparation for meeting the Savior at the end of our lives and at the final judgement. Such prayer effectively feeds an Advent faith in eucharistic mode.

Maybe more surprising is the impact the church year has on the way Scripture is employed in our worship. This is well summed up by theologian Fritz West, who contends that the very structure of our lectionary is driven by the design and flow of the liturgical year. He calls this the "catholic principle."[1] This principle recognizes that in our tradition, not only is Scripture interpreted through the liturgy, but the biblical texts are fundamentally shaped and even selected because of the cycle of feasts and seasons. In a parallel way, the noted biblical scholar Dianne Bergant recognizes that the liturgical year, with its rhythm of seasons and feasts, is a key interpretive lens for an appropriate understanding and subsequent preaching of the weekly lectionary texts.[2]

Given the impact of the liturgical year on the celebration of Mass, it seems obvious and necessary that it should have a similar influence on the devotions drawn from that central eucharistic liturgy. There are multiple and simple ways this can be achieved. As with the main sanctuary space used for Mass, any chapels or other rooms employed for eucharistic devotions should also be decorated in the spirit of the season. Changing the environment for eucharistic devotions connects such practices with the central eucharistic action that ordinarily occurs with similar seasonal accents.

In the same vein, to the extent that there is music or readings connected with the devotions, these too could easily be selected for their seasonal resonance. Staying with Advent, for example, "O Come, O Come, Emmanuel" is a particularly apt piece of music for eucharistic adoration. The very name "Emmanuel" means "God is with us." That is precisely what believers assert in a distinctive way by befriending God's presence in the Blessed Sacrament. The multiple petitions in that prayer—to disperse gloom, open heaven wide, and assure victory over death—recommend it as a useful text to ponder in eucharistic adoration, even apart from any singing of the hymn. Having simple prayer cards with this text in spaces frequented for eucharistic adoration is one way to make this material accessible. Moreover, in light of COVID-19, many of our churches are more comfortable with online resources and apps. Having such a text digitally available promotes a true liturgical devotion faithfully aligned to the church's eucharistic liturgy.

When it comes to the readings, sometimes short snippets from designated lectionary texts may be the way to go. Often in eucharistic contemplation, a few lines or even a few words from a prayer or scripture are sufficient for nourishing meditation in the presence of the reserved sacrament. Continuing the Advent example, that season's first readings are especially rich in prophetic references to Christ's coming. Many of these echo prayer instincts that well up within us in the presence of the Blessed Sacrament. A few examples are:

- "Come, let us climb the LORD's mountain, / to the house of the God of Jacob, / that he may instruct us in his ways, / and we may walk in his paths" (First Sunday of Advent, Cycle A—Isaiah 2:3);

- "Fear not to cry out / and say to the cities of Judah: / Here is your God!" (Second Sunday of Advent, Cycle B—Isaiah 40:9);

- "The LORD, your God, is in your midst, / a mighty savior; / he will rejoice over you with gladness / and renew you in his love" (Third Sunday of Advent, Cycle C—Zephaniah 3:17);

- "Who can ascend the mountain of the LORD? / or who may stand in his holy place? / One whose hands are sinless, whose heart is clean, / who desires not what is vain" (Fourth Sunday of Advent, Cycle A—Responsorial Psalm 24:3-4).

Again, simple prayer cards, pamphlets or digital postings of such resources will provide enriched biblical and liturgical foundations for eucharistic adoration and devotions. They will also fulfill the council's mandate to ensure that such devotions both flow from and lead back to the sacrifice of the Mass which lies at the very heart of our faith and prayer life.

Preaching, Exhortations, and Catechesis: Parallel to Vatican II's great achievement of restoring the Word of God to prominence in our worship and theologizing was its revitalization of the preaching event. While sermons were ubiquitous before the council, they often ignored the readings that had just been proclaimed. For this and other reasons, they were not true homilies. Instead, the preaching frequently followed some catechetical or dogmatic syllabus, for example: a series of exhortations about various virtues or an exposition of the central tenets of the creed. It was quite common for these instructions to treat topics that were extraneous to the liturgy itself. The liturgical disconnect between the sermon and eucharistic worship is reflected in the very structure of the Tridentine Roman Missal (1570), which surprisingly makes no mention of preaching in its Order of Mass. Thus, central preaching events often moved outside the eucharistic sacrifice and instead became key elements in parish missions or during popular devotions, including Benediction of the Blessed Sacrament.

The recovery of the ancient genre of the homily as an integral element in the liturgy was a twentieth-century phenomenon. This historical and theological rehabilitation of this unique form of preaching culminated in Vatican II's teaching that

> by means of the homily, the mysteries of the faith and the guiding principles of the christian life are expounded from the sacred text during the course of the liturgical year. The homily is strongly recommended since it forms part of the liturgy itself. In fact, at those Masses which are celebrated on Sundays and holidays of obligation, with the people assisting, it should not be omitted except for a serious reason. (*CSL* 52)

The connection between Scripture and the homily in the celebration of the Mass finds resonance in the instructions for celebrating eucharistic exposition and adoration. Consequently, the Rite of Eucharistic Exposition and Benediction notes not only that there should be readings from Scripture but also that these should be accompanied by "a homily or brief exhortations to develop a better understanding of the eucharistic mystery" (95). The canonical distinction here is that a homily can only be delivered by an ordained person, while others can offer an exhortation.

The guidance to offer such preaching or teaching in order to enable the faithful to develop a better understanding of the Eucharist calls to mind a revered form of liturgical instruction in our tradition: mystagogy. Some may be familiar with this term from the Rite of Christian Initiation of Adults. In that ritual, mystagogy is largely defined as a period of catechesis that needs to occur after the elect have been fully initiated (244). At the same time, that rite acknowledges a broader understanding of the term as a kind of theological reflection upon the rites themselves. Thus, it teaches that mystagogy introduces the newly initiated "into a fuller and more effective understanding of the mysteries . . . above all through their experience of the sacraments they have received" (245). In a parallel teaching, the *Catechism of the Catholic Church* frames mystagogy in terms of liturgical catechesis whose purpose is to initiate people into the mystery of Christ. This is achieved by "proceeding from the visible to the invisible, from the sign to the thing signified, from the sacraments to the mysteries" (1075).

Many Roman Catholics are initiated into eucharistic adoration and parallel devotions through practice. For example, some of us were taught at a very early age "how" to make a visit to the Blessed Sacrament as well as "what" prayers to say during such visits. However, we are seldom taught how to reflect on the significance of these visits or other such eucharistic practices. It is one thing to learn a pious practice by watching or participating. It is quite another to develop the desire and to acquire the skills to reflect on the meaning of such practices for Christian living.

Preaching or offering exhortations within eucharistic devotions, as well as sustained liturgical catechesis on such practices, is an essential pastoral effort that helps the faithful experience the fullness of graces from these experiences. Some of these graces and their lived realizations are richly illuminated by Holy Communion and Worship of the Eucharist outside Mass:

- a disposition toward "sacramental and spiritual communion" (80),

- a spirit of deep gratitude for Christ's gifts (80),

- a willingness to "pour out their hearts" for others (80),

- a commitment to "pray for the peace and salvation of the world" (80),

- an increase in faith, hope, and love (80),

- the strength to lead whole lives nourished by the eucharistic gift (81),

- a concern with good deeds (81),

- a willingness "to imbue the world with the Christian spirit" (81), and

- a commitment to be "witnesses of Christ" in the midst of human society (81).

Participating in eucharistic adoration and devotions will not necessarily ensure that one will develop a healthy and life-giving eucharistic spirituality. While preaching, exhortations, and liturgical catechesis will not guarantee this either, they are historically tested and magisterially endorsed aids for such development. This is especially true if our eucharistic practices are to be renewed and inspirited in the spirit of Vatican II. For this to occur, "such a renewal must be imbued with a pedagogical awareness" (*Directory on Popular Piety and the Liturgy*, 12). Preaching practices in mystagogical mode undoubtedly contribute to such an awareness.

Active Contemplation: One of the most heralded achievements of the twentieth-century liturgical reform was its emphasis on the active participation of the assembly. The liturgical constitution pointedly held this up as the litmus test for evaluating the effectiveness of the reform. In one of the most quoted paragraphs of that document, the council fathers taught:

> In the restoration and development of the sacred liturgy the full and active participation by all the people is the paramount concern, for it is the primary, indeed the indispensable source from which the faithful are to derive the true Christian spirit. Therefore, in all their apostolic activity, pastors of souls should energetically set about achieving it through the requisite formation." (*CSL* 14)

Given the powerful language here—especially the affirmation that the full, conscious, and active participation of the people is the paramount concern in the liturgical reform—a central question remains when it comes to eucharistic devotions. Some forms of these devotions, particularly practices such as eucharistic processions and even Benediction, allow for multiple forms of active participation. These rituals invite various options for singing, responses, and change of posture that combine for multiple opportunities for spoken and embodied forms of participation. However, when it comes to adoration, visits to the Blessed Sacrament, and other such eucharistic devotions, how does one achieve active participation?

One of the most common ways to characterize prayer before the Blessed Sacrament and its various forms of adoration is as "contemplation." Pope Benedict XVI affirmed this in *Sacramentum Caritatis* (The Sacrament of Charity) when he applauded various associations and confraternities devoted to Eucharist adoration "as a leaven of contemplation for the whole church" (67). Contemplation is sometimes imagined as the opposite of active participation. A classic example of this perspective is the anonymous fourteenth-century work, *The Cloud of Unknowing*.[3] The work consists of a series of letters written by an English monk to his student or disciple. Knowing God, from this teacher's perspective, does not come through gifts of insight nor actions of the intellect. Rather it happens through a kind of love stripped of all thought. This mystical immersion leads to a kind of darkness. This cloud is between the believer and God, and the believer is urged not to presume to understand this cloud through reason or understanding. Rather, there is an invitation for the believer to remain in this darkness as long as possible, in the hope of feeling God in the sweetness of love.[4]

While the author of *The Cloud of Unknowing* does not disparage active ministry, it is clearly not the primary value in these letters. This becomes clear when the author draws a strong distinction between the active and contemplative life. The model for this distinction is Luke's account of Jesus at the home of Martha and Mary (Luke 10:38-42). While Martha's service is deemed good and helpful for her salvation, it is clear that

Mary's contemplative stance is more honorable.[5] In a similar way, contemplation in the presence of the Blessed Sacrament is highly prized by many. In the words of a former student, "I like being there, undisturbed; it takes me out of the chaos of my daily life."

There are, however, other ways to think about contemplation. In my own Franciscan tradition, St. Francis of Assisi was a sainted mystic who nonetheless rebuilt churches, embraced lepers, calmed marauding wolves, and engaged a Muslim Sultan in a mutually respectful dialogue. For many in the history of Christian mysticism, contemplation catapults them into action, ministry, and the world. While Francis never crafted a method for others to follow in his mystical gift, his dear friend did. Widely regarded as the cofounder of the Franciscan movement, St. Clare of Assisi longed to share Francis's new vision of religious life that combined contemplation and action. Unfortunately, because of the strictures of the age, she lived out her ministry from 1212 until her death in 1253 as a cloistered nun. In the process, she founded what is now known as the Order of Poor Clares. Unlike Francis, Clare did write with some specificity about her own process of prayer and contemplation. While her method is not contained in one single document, reading through her letters—especially those penned to her own blood sister, venerated as Agnes of Prague (d. 1282)—one can discern a very clear pattern for contemplation. The four steps are imaged in the presence of a mirror, especially a mirror suspended on the wood of the cross. According to Clare, first you gaze as you fix your attention on the cross. Then you reflect, engaging your imagination and feelings that rise up when seeing such holy humility. Next you contemplate, becoming present while pouring yourself out in the presence of such eternal charity and divine emptying. Finally, there is a call to response or imitation in which you are moved to imitate the same kinds of humility, charity, and holy emptying for others.[6]

This deeply absorbing and wholly authentic form of contemplation has a dual dynamic or movement. As described by the Poor Clare theologian Edith van den Goorbergh:

> There is a visible movement from the *outside to the inside*. Clare describes a process by which contemplation is internalized: the praying person is touched by something, she observes, and as the gaze intensifies so the inner involvement is increased. Our surrender to that at which we gaze develops. The growing intensity of this gazing results in a heartfelt contemplation and this, in its turn, initiates a returning dynamic from *the inside to the outside*. . . . a fervent longing to follow him.[7]

In a similar way, eucharistic adoration and its allied devotions are an invitation to move from the "outside" and highly participatory experience of the Mass to an internal contemplation of the holy humility of God in Christ who chooses to be present through those most unassuming elements of bread and a cup of wine. This contemplative move is not a withdrawal from the call to full, conscious, and active participation. Rather, it is a highly graced internalization in a process that allows us to bask in the radiant grace of divine presence before returning to that challenging baptismal mission to live authentic eucharistic lives. This is the form of active contemplation necessary for a credible eucharistic spirituality. If we make only the initial interior move from the outside to the inside, without any intention or zeal to return to a fully inspired life of eucharistic charity, then we short-circuit the power and the purpose of these critical pious practices. We are not invited simply to stay with Jesus in retreat from the field hospital that Pope Francis calls the church to be.[8] Rather, we momentarily rest in the Divine Presence so that we can launch back with new vigor and commitment into the world whose belovedness was revealed by the Only Begotten (John 3:16).

Summary

Eucharistic devotions, in all of their rich diversity, are an admitted treasure of the Catholic Christian tradition. This closing reflection on principles and guidelines for pastoral practice does not question the value of this treasure. Instead, it asks how such a gift will be safeguarded. Some treasures, like bars of gold bullion or stashes of precious sapphires and rubies, need to be protected by being sealed in unbreachable vaults surrounded by layers of impenetrable security. The Jesus treasure offered in the Eucharist, however, is not that kind of treasure. Rather, it is that pearl of great price that must be accessible, shared and freely given—as was the very ministry of Jesus, who bequeathed the eucharistic gift to us. That does not mean, however, that we are careless with this holy abundance. Rather, we safeguard this precious gift with thoughtful preparation, careful enactment, and sustained evaluation and renewal. In so doing, we refresh this ancient gift for the unforeseen generations who will find it in sustenance, grace, and a pathway to eternal life. Thus, in the spirit of St. Paul, we keep alert in our prayer with that attitude of thanksgiving (Col 4:2), always learning anew how we might become what we reverence and what we eat.

Notes

Introduction

1. Quotations of Vatican II documents are taken from Austin Flannery, ed., *Vatican Council II: Constitutions, Decrees, Declarations; The Basic Sixteen Documents* (Collegeville, MN: Liturgical Press, 2014).

Chapter One

1. Robert Wilken, *The Myth of Christian Beginnings* (Notre Dame: University of Notre Dame Press, 1971).

2. James D. Whitehead and Evelyn Eaton Whitehead, *Method in Ministry: Theological Reflection and Christian Ministry*, rev. ed. (Kansas City: Sheed and Ward, 1995).

3. Justin Martyr, *First Apology*, 67.

4. Basil the Great, *Letter* 93.

5. Augustine, *Commentary on Psalm 98*, 98.9.

6. Cyril of Jerusalem, *Catechesis*, 23.21.

7. John Chrysostom, *Homilies on the Gospel of Matthew*, 7:6.

8. Nathan Mitchell, *Cult and Controversy: The Worship of the Eucharist Outside Mass* (New York: Pueblo, 1982), 46.

9. Robert Taft, "Is There Devotion to the Holy Eucharist in the Christian East?," *Worship* 80 (2006): 221.

10. James Russell, *The Germanization of Early Medieval Christianity: A Sociohistorical Approach to Religious Transformation* (New York: Oxford University Press, 1994), 191.

11. Gregory of Nazianzus, *Oration*, 8:18.

12. Charles Freeman, *Holy Bones, Holy Dust: How Relics Shaped the History of Medieval Europe* (New Haven: Yale University Press, 2011), especially chap. 6.

13. Theodoret, *Ecclesiastical History*, 1:17.

14. Egeria, 36.4

15. Patrick Geary, *Furta Sacra: Thefts of Relics in the Central Middle Ages*, rev. ed. (Princeton, NJ: Princeton University Press, 1990).

16. Freeman, *Holy Bones, Holy Dust*, 5.

17. Ibid., chap. 6.

18. Patrick Geary, "Sacred Commodities: The Circulation of Medieval Relics," in *The Social Life of Things: Commodities in Cultural Perspective*, ed. Arjun Appadurai (Cambridge: Cambridge University Press, 1986), 187.

19. Henri de Lubac, *Corpus Mysticum: The Eucharist and the Church in the Middle Ages*, trans. Gemma Simmonds, ed. Laurence Paul Hemming and Susan Frank Parsons (Notre Dame: University of Notre Dame Press, 2006).

20. Augustine, *Sermon 272*, trans. Nathan Mitchell, *Assembly* 23, no. 2 (1997): 14.

21. Gary Macy, *The Theologies of the Eucharist in the Early Scholastic Period: A Study of the Salvific Function of the Sacrament according to the Theologians c.1080–c.1220* (Oxford: Clarendon Press, 1984).

22. Ibid., 88.

23. Mitchell, *Cult and Controversy*, 165.

24. Macy, *Theologies of the Eucharist*, 89.

25. *Regularis Concordia*, 65.

26. Macy, *Theologies of the Eucharist*, 88.

27. Herbert Thurston, "The Early Cultus of the Blessed Sacrament," *Month* 109 (1907): 388.

28. *Regularis Concordia*, 46–51.

29. Mitchell, *Cult and Controversy*, 133–34.

30. Johannes von Marienwerder, *The Life of Dorothea von Montau: A Fourteenth-Century Recluse*, trans. Ute Stargardt, Studies in Women and Religion (Lewiston, NY: Edwin Mellen Press, 1997), 39:169.

31. Giovanni Domenico Mansi, *Sacrorum conciliorum nova et amplissima collection* (Paris: H. Welter, 1901–27), 32:149.

32. Eamon Duffy, *The Stripping of the Altars: Traditional Religion in England, 1400–1450*, 2nd ed. (New Haven: Yale University Press, 2005), 95.

33. James L. Connolly, "Benediction of the Blessed Sacrament," *The Ecclesiastical Review* 85, no. 5 (November 1931): 455.

34. Ibid., 459.

35. *Ancrene Wisse*, ed. Robert Hasenfratz (Kalamazoo, MI: Medieval Institute Publications, 2000).

36. Ibid., lines 11–29, 176–86.

37. Nathan Mitchell, "The Struggle of Religious Women for Eucharist," *Benedictines* 52 (1999): 12–25.

38. Ibid., 18.

39. Macy, *Theologies of the Eucharist*, 90.

40. Mechthild of Magdeburg, *The Flowing Light of the Godhead*, trans. Frank Tobin, The Classics of Western Spirituality (New York: Paulist Press, 1998), 111.

41. Macy, *Theologies of the Eucharist*, 84.

42. Amy Nelson Burnett, "The Social History of Communion and the Reformation of the Eucharist," *Past & Present* 211 (2011): 84.

43. Barbara Walters, Vincent Corrigan, and Peter Rickets, *The Feast of Corpus Christi* (University Park, PA: Pennsylvania State University Press, 2006), 7.

44. Miri Rubin, Corpus Christi: *The Eucharist in Late Medieval Culture* (Cambridge: Cambridge University Press, 1991), 353.

45. Maxwell Johnson, *The Church in Act* (Minneapolis: Augsburg Fortress, 2015), 89–92.

46. Ibid., 103.

47. Augustine, *On the Trinity*, 4:6.

48. Josef Jungmann, "Die Andacht der Vierzig Stunden und das heilige Grab," *Liturgisches Jahrbuch* 2 (1952): 195.

49. Ibid., 184.

50. Egidio Picucci, "Le Quarantore nei documenti pontifici e nella pietà del Popolo di Dio," *L'Osservatore Romano*, edizione quotidiana (2–3 May 2005).

51. Herbert Thurston, "Forty Hours' Devotion," in *The Catholic Encyclopedia*, ed. Charles Herbermann (New York: Robert Appleton, 1909), 6:151.

52. Charles Borromeo, *Acta Ecclesiae Mediolanensis* (Milan, 1599), 581, https://archive.org/details/actaecclesiaemed01cath/page/n3/mode/2up.

53. Joseph McMahon, "Perpetual Adoration," in *The Catholic Encyclopediaa*, ed. Charles Herbermann (New York: Robert Appleton, 1907), 1:154.

54. Nathan Mitchell, "Eucharistic Devotion," in *New Catholic Encyclopedia*, 2nd ed. (Detroit: Thomas-Gale, 2003), 6:425.

55. Jules Corblet, *Histoire dogmatique, liturgique et archéologique du sacrement de l'eucharistie* (Paris: Société Générale de Librairie Catholique, 1886), 2:441.

56. Ibid., 441.

57. Nathan Mitchell, "Eucharistic Adoration Revisited," *Worship* 83, no. 5 (2009): 463.

58. Ibid., 466.

59. Ibid., 469.

60. Mitchell, *Cult and Controversy*, 182–83.

61. Connolly, "Benediction of the Blessed Sacrament," 453–54.

62. *Rituale Romanum*, 71, 312–13.

63. Mitchell, *Cult and Controversy*, 201.

64. Margaret Mary Alacoque, *The Autobiography*, trans. Sisters of the Visitation (Charlotte, NC: TAN Books, 2012 [1930]), 57, 96.

65. Francis Costa, "Holy Hour," in *New Catholic Encyclopedia*, 2nd ed. (Detroit: Thomas-Gale, 2003), 7:30.

66. Benedict Groeschel and James Monti, *In the Presence of the Lord: The History, Theology and Psychology of Eucharistic Devotion* (Huntington, IN: Our Sunday Visitor, 1996), 252.

67. Mitchell, "Eucharistic Devotion," 435.

68. Alphonsus Liguori, *Visits to the Blessed Sacrament and to Blessed Mary*, trans. Eugene Grimm (Vancouver: Eremitical Press, 2010), 25.

69. Massimo Faggioli, *True Reform: Liturgy and Ecclesiology in* Sacrosanctum Concilium (Collegeville, MN: Liturgical Press, 2012), 11.

70. Ibid., 149, 153.

71. Mitchell, *Cult and Controversy*, 201.

72. Groeschel and Monti, *In the Presence of the Lord*, 275.

73. *L'Osservatore Romano*, "Statutes Approved for the Association of Perpetual Eucharistic Adoration" (5 August 1991): 8.

74. Groeschel and Monti, *In the Presence of the Lord*, 284.

75. Congregation for Divine Worship and the Discipline of the Sacraments, *Directory on Popular Piety and the Liturgy: Principles and Guidelines* (Vatican City, 2001), http://www.vatican.va/roman_curia/congregations /ccdds/documents/rc_con_ccdds_doc_20020513_vers-direttorio_en .html.

Chapter Two

1. Augustine, *Sermon 272*, trans. Nathan Mitchell, *Assembly* 23, no. 2 (1997): 14.

2. *Catechism of the Catholic Church*, 2nd ed. (United States Catholic Conference—Libreria Editrice Vaticana, 1997).

3. Nathan Mitchell, "The Struggle of Religious Women for Eucharist," *Benedictines* 52 (1999): 25.

4. David J. Bosch, *Transforming Mission* (Maryknoll, NY: Orbis, 1991), 389–90.

5. Stephen Bevans and Roger Schroeder, *Constants in Context: A Theology of Mission for Today* (Maryknoll, NY: Orbis, 2004), 288.

6. John Paul II, General Audience, 21 June 2000, https://m.vatican.va /content/john-paul-ii/en/audiences/2000/documents/hf_jp-ii_aud _20000621.html.

7. Peter Turksson, "Adoration as the Foundation of Social Justice," in *From Eucharistic Adoration to Evangelization*, ed. Alcuin Reid (London: Burns and Oates, 2012), 174, n. 15.

8. Benedict XVI, *Sacramentum Caritatis*, 22 February 2007, http://www .vatican.va/content/benedict-xvi/en/apost_exhortations/documents /hf_ben-xvi_exh_20070222_sacramentum-caritatis.html.

9. Christopher Ruddy, "Pope and Abbot," *America* (22 May 2006), https://www.americamagazine.org/issue/573/article/pope-and-abbot.

10. Luis Antonio Tagle, "L'adoration authentique," *Lumen Vitae* 64, no. 3 (2009): 298.

11. Francis, *The Joy of the Gospel*, 24 November 2013, https://www.vatican.va/content/francesco/en/apost_exhortations/documents/papa-francesco_esortazione-ap_20131124_evangelii-gaudium.html.

12. Joris Geldhof, "Fruit of the Earth, Work of Human Hands, Bread of Life: The *Ordo Missae* on Creation and the World," in *Full of Your Glory: Liturgy, Cosmos, Creation*, ed. Teresa Berger (Collegeville, MN: Liturgical Press, 2019), 259.

13. Arthur Peacocke, *Creation and the World of Science: The Re-Shaping of Belief* (Oxford: Oxford University Press, 2004 [1979]), 301.

14. Benedict XVI, *Spe Salvi* 28, 30 November 2007, http://www.vatican.va/content/benedict-xvi/en/encyclicals/documents/hf_ben-xvi_enc_20071130_spe-salvi.html.

15. John D. Zizioulas, "Ecological Asceticism: A Cultural Revolution," *Sourozh* 67 (1997): 22–25.

16. Ilia Delio, *A Franciscan View of Creation: Learning to Live in a Sacramental World*, ed. Joseph P. Chinnici, Franciscan Heritage Series (Mansfield, OH: Book Masters, 2003), 11:7.

17. Delio, *Franciscan View of Creation*, 21–32.

18. Francis, *Laudato Si'* (On Care for Our Common Home; translated literally from Italian as "Praise be to you [my Lord]"), 24 May 2015, https://www.vatican.va/content/francesco/en/encyclicals/documents/papa-francesco_20150524_enciclica-laudato-si.html.

19. Pierre Teilhard de Chardin, *The Divine Milieu* (London: Collins, 1960), 126.

20. Karl Rahner, "An Earthly Mysticism," in *The Great Church Year: The Best of Karl Rahner's Homilies, Sermons, and Meditations*, ed. Albert Raffelt and Harvey Egan, 239 (New York: Crossroad, 1994).

Chapter Three

1. Lionel Obadia, "Spirituality," in *The Wiley-Blackwell Encyclopedia of Social Theory*, ed. Bryan S. Turner and others, 5 vols. (2017), https://doi.org/10.1002/9781118430873.est0373.

2. For example, see Sandra Schneiders, "Spirituality in the Academy," *Theological Studies* 50 (1989): 676–97.

3. See, for example, Karl Rahner, *The Mystical Way in Everyday Life*, trans. and ed. Annemarie Kidder (Maryknoll, NY: Orbis Books, 2010).

4. Teresa Berger, *@Worship: Liturgical Practices in Digital Worlds*, Liturgy, Worship and Society Series (New York: Routledge, 2018), 19–20.

5. Anthony Kelly, "The Body of Christ: Amen!: The Expanding Incarnation," *Theological Studies* 71, no. 4 (2010): 802.

6. Francis, Angelus, 3 January 2021, http://www.vatican.va/content/francesco/en/angelus/2021/documents/papa-francesco_angelus_20210103.html.

7. Francis, Vigil of Pentecost Address, 18 May 2013, http://www.vatican.va/content/francesco/en/speeches/2013/may/documents/papa-francesco_20130518_veglia-pentecoste.html.

8. Monika Hellwig, *Eucharist and the Hungers of the World* (Kansas City: Sheed and Ward, 1992), 10–11.

9. Joan Ridley, *In the Presence: The Spirituality of Eucharistic Adoration* (Liguori, MO: Liguori, 2010), 55.

10. Gerhard Lohfink, *Jesus of Nazareth: What He Wanted, Who He Was*, trans. Linda M. Maloney (Collegeville, MN: Liturgical Press, 2012), 74.

11. Pius XII, *Mediator Dei*, 20 November 1947, http://www.vatican.va/content/pius-xii/en/encyclicals/documents/hf_p-xii_enc_20111947_mediator-dei.html.

12. Edward Schillebeeckx, *Christ, The Sacrament of the Encounter with God* (New York: Sheed and Ward, 1963).

13. Claude-Marie Barbour, "Seeking Justice and Shalom in the City," *International Review of Mission* 73 (1984): 304.

14. Stephen Bevans, "God Inside Out: Toward a Missionary Theology of the Holy Spirit," *International Bulletin of Missionary Research* 22, no. 3 (1998): 102.

15. Regis J. Armstrong, J. A. Wayne Hellmann, and William Short, eds., *Francis of Assisi: Early Documents*, vol. 1: *The Saint* (New York: New City Press, 1999), 118.

16. Joseph Bernardin, "A Consistent Ethic of Life: An American-Catholic-Dialogue," 6 December 1983, https://www.priestsforlife.org/magisterium/bernardingannon.html.

17. Joseph Bernardin, "A Consistent Ethic of Life," 11 March 1984, https://www.priestsforlife.org/magisterium/bernardinwade.html.

18. John Paul II and Bartholomew, Common Declaration on Environmental Ethics, 10 June 2002, https://www.vatican.va/content/john-paul-ii/en/speeches/2002/june/documents/hf_jp-ii_spe_20020610_venice-declaration.html.

19. Michael Rosenzweig, *Win-Win Ecology: How the Earth's Species Can Survive in the Midst of Human Enterprise* (New York: Oxford University Press, 2003), 7.

20. David Warners, Michael Ryskamp, and Randall Van Dragt, "Reconciliation Ecology: A New Paradigm for Advancing Creation Care," *Perspectives on Science and Faith* 66, no. 4 (2014): 224.

Chapter Four

1. Fritz West, *Scripture and Memory: The Ecumenical Hermeneutic of the Three-Year Lectionaries* (Collegeville, MN: Liturgical Press, 1997), 47–52.

2. Dianne Bergant and Richard Fragomeni, *Preaching the New Lectionary: Year A* (Collegeville, MN: Liturgical Press, 2001), vii.

3. *The Cloud of Unknowing*, trans. A. C. Spearing (London: Penguin, 2002).

4. Ibid., 26.

5. Ibid., 50–51.

6. Regis Armstrong, ed. and trans., *Clare of Assisi: Early Documents* (New York: New City Press, 2006), 55–57.

7. Edith van den Goorbergh, "Clare's Prayer as a Spiritual Journey," *Greyfriars Review* 10, no. 3 (1996): 285.

8. Antonio Spadaro, "A Big Heart Open to God: An Interview with Pope Francis," *America* (30 September 2013), https://www.americamagazine.org/faith/2013/09/30/big-heart-open-god-interview-pope-francis.

Bibliography

Alacoque, Margaret Mary. *The Autobiography.* Translated by Sisters of the Visitation. Charlotte, NC: TAN Books, 2012 (1930).

Ancrene Wisse. Edited by Robert Hasenfratz. Kalamazoo, MI: Medieval Institute Publications, 2000.

The Anglican Service Book: A Traditional Language Adaptation of the 1979 Book of Common Prayer. Rosemont, PA: Church of the Good Shepherd, 1991.

Armstrong, Regis J., ed. and trans. *Clare of Assisi: Early Documents.* New York: New City Press, 2006.

Armstrong, Regis J., J. A. Wayne Hellmann, and William Short, eds. *Francis of Assisi: Early Documents.* Vol. 1: *The Saint.* New York: New City Press, 1999.

Augustine. *Sermon 272.* Translated by Nathan Mitchell. *Assembly* 23, no. 2 (1997): 14.

Barbour, Claude-Marie. "Seeking Justice and Shalom in the City." *International Review of Mission* 73 (1984): 303–9.

Benedict XVI, Pope. *Sacramentum Caritatis.* 22 February 2007. https://www.vatican.va/content/benedict-xvi/en/apost_exhortations/documents/hf_ben-xvi_exh_20070222_sacramentum-caritatis.html.

———. *Spe Salvi.* 30 November 2007. http://www.vatican.va/content/benedict-xvi/en/encyclicals/documents/hf_ben-xvi_enc_20071130_spe-salvi.html.

Bergant, Dianne, and Richard Fragomeni. *Preaching the New Lectionary: Year A.* Collegeville, MN: Liturgical Press, 2001.

Berger, Teresa. *@Worship: Liturgical Practices in Digital Worlds.* Liturgy, Worship and Society Series. New York: Routledge, 2018.

Bernardin, Joseph. "A Consistent Ethic of Life." 11 March 1984. https://www.priestsforlife.org/magisterium/bernardinwade.html.

———. "A Consistent Ethic of Life: An American-Catholic-Dialogue." 6 December 1983. https://www.priestsforlife.org/magisterium/bernardingannon.html.

Bevans, Stephen. "God Inside Out: Toward a Missionary Theology of the Holy Spirit." *International Bulletin of Missionary Research* 22, no. 3 (1998): 102–5.

Bevans, Stephen, and Roger Schroeder. *Constants in Context: A Theology of Mission for Today.* Maryknoll, NY: Orbis, 2004.

Borromeo, Charles. *Acta Ecclesiae Mediolanensis.* Milan, 1599. https://archive.org/details/actaecclesiaemed01cath/page/n3/mode/2up.

Bosch, David J. *Transforming Mission.* Maryknoll, NY: Orbis, 1991.

Burnett, Amy Nelson. "The Social History of Communion and the Reformation of the Eucharist." *Past & Present* 211 (2011): 77–119.

Catechism of the Catholic Church. 2nd ed. United States Catholic Conference—Libreria Editrice Vaticana, 1997.

The Cloud of Unknowing. Translated by A. C. Spearing. London: Penguin, 2002.

Congregation for Divine Worship and the Discipline of the Sacraments. *Directory on Popular Piety and the Liturgy: Principles and Guidelines.* Vatican City: 2001. http://www.vatican.va/roman_curia/congregations/ccdds/documents/rc_con_ccdds_doc_20020513_vers-direttorio_en.html.

Connolly, James L. "Benediction of the Blessed Sacrament." *The Ecclesiastical Review* 85, no. 5 (November 1931): 449–62.

Corblet, Jules. *Histoire dogmatique, liturgique et archéologique du sacrement de l'eucharistie.* Vol 2. Paris: Société Générale de Librairie Catholique, 1886.

Costa, Francis. "Holy Hour" (7:30). In *New Catholic Encyclopedia.* 2nd ed., 15 vols. Detroit: Thomas-Gale, 2003.

de Chardin, Pierre Teilhard. *The Divine Milieu.* London: Collins, 1960.

de Lubac, Henri. *Corpus Mysticum: The Eucharist and the Church in the Middle Ages.* Translated by Gemma Simmonds, edited by Laurence Paul Hemming and Susan Frank Parsons. Notre Dame: University of Notre Dame Press, 2006.

Delio, Ilia. *A Franciscan View of Creation: Learning to Live in a Sacramental World.* Edited by Joseph P. Chinnici. Franciscan Heritage Series, vol. 11. Mansfield, OH: Book Masters, 2003.

Duffy, Eamon. *The Stripping of the Altars: Traditional Religion in England, 1400–1450.* 2nd ed. New Haven: Yale University Press, 2005.

Faggioli, Massimo. *True Reform: Liturgy and Ecclesiology in* Sacrosanctum Concilium. Collegeville, MN: Liturgical Press, 2012.

Flannery, Austin, ed. *Vatican Council II: Constitutions, Decrees, Declarations; The Basic Sixteen Documents.* Collegeville, MN: Liturgical Press, 2014.

Foley, Edward. "Sharing the Cup: A Way of Being in the World." *Emmanuel* 107, no. 3 (April 2001): 147–51.

Francis, Pope. Angelus. 3 January 2021. http://www.vatican.va /content/francesco/en/angelus/2021/documents/papa -francesco_angelus_20210103.html.

———. *The Joy of the Gospel.* 24 November 2013. https://www.vatican .va/content/francesco/en/apost_exhortations/documents /papa-francesco_esortazione-ap_20131124_evangelii-gaudium .html.

———. *Laudato Si'.* 24 May 2015. https://www.vatican.va/content/ francesco/en/encyclicals/documents/papa-francesco _20150524_enciclica-laudato-si.html.

———. Vigil of Pentecost Address. 18 May 2013. http://www .vatican.va/content/francesco/en/speeches/2013/may /documents/papa-francesco_20130518_veglia-pentecoste .html.

Freeman, Charles. *Holy Bones, Holy Dust: How Relics Shaped the History of Medieval Europe.* New Haven: Yale University Press, 2011.

Geary, Patrick. *Furta Sacra: Thefts of Relics in the Central Middle Ages.* Rev. ed. Princeton, NJ: Princeton University Press, 1990.

———. "Sacred Commodities: The Circulation of Medieval Relics." In *The Social Life of Things: Commodities in Cultural Perspective,* edited by Arjun Appadurai, 169–91. Cambridge: Cambridge University Press, 1986.

Geldhof, Joris. "Fruit of the Earth, Work of Human Hands, Bread of Life: The *Ordo Missae* on Creation and the World." In *Full of Your Glory: Liturgy, Cosmos, Creation,* edited by Teresa Berger, 245–65. Collegeville, MN: Liturgical Press, 2019.

Groeschel, Benedict, and James Monti. *In the Presence of the Lord: The History, Theology and Psychology of Eucharistic Devotion.* Huntington, IN: Our Sunday Visitor, 1996.

Hellwig, Monika. *Eucharist and the Hungers of the World.* Kansas City: Sheed and Ward, 1992.

Holy Communion and Worship of the Eucharist outside Mass (pp. 631–98). In *The Rites of the Catholic Church: Volume One.* Collegeville, MN: Liturgical Press, 1990.

John Paul II, Pope St. General Audience. 21 June 2000. http://www.vatican.va/content/john-paul-ii/en/audiences/2000/documents/hf_jp-ii_aud_20000621.html.

John Paul II, Pope St., and Ecumenical Patriarch Bartholomew. Common Declaration on Environmental Ethics. 10 June 2002. https://www.vatican.va/content/john-paul-ii/en/speeches/2002/june/documents/hf_jp-ii_spe_20020610_venice-declaration.html.

Johnson, Maxwell. *The Church in Act.* Minneapolis: Augsburg Fortress, 2015.

Jungmann, Josef. "Die Andacht der Vierzig Stunden und das heilige Grab." *Liturgisches Jahrbuch* 2 (1952): 184–98.

Kelly, Anthony. "The Body of Christ: Amen!: The Expanding Incarnation." *Theological Studies* 71, no. 4 (2010): 792–816.

Liguori, Alphonsus. *Visits to the Blessed Sacrament and to Blessed Mary.* Translated by Eugene Grimm. Vancouver: Eremitical Press, 2010.

Lohfink, Gerhard. *Jesus of Nazareth: What He Wanted, Who He Was.* Translated by Linda M. Maloney. Collegeville, MN: Liturgical Press, 2012.

Macy, Gary. *The Theologies of the Eucharist in the Early Scholastic Period: A Study of the Salvific Function of the Sacrament according to the Theologians c.1080–c.1220.* Oxford: Clarendon Press, 1984.

Mansi, Giovanni Domenico. *Sacrorum conciliorum nova et amplissima collectio.* Paris: H. Welter, 1901–27.

McMahon, Joseph. "Perpetual Adoration" (1:152–54). In *The Catholic Encyclopedia,* edited by Charles Herbermann. 15 vols. New York: Robert Appleton, 1907.

Mechthild of Magdeburg. *The Flowing Light of the Godhead.* Translated by Frank Tobin. The Classics of Western Spirituality. New York: Paulist Press, 1998.

Mitchell, Nathan. *Cult and Controversy: The Worship of the Eucharist Outside Mass.* New York: Pueblo, 1982.

———. "Eucharistic Adoration Revisited." *Worship* 83, no. 5 (2009): 457–71.

———. "Eucharistic Devotion" (6:434–36). In *New Catholic Encyclopedia.* 2nd ed., 15 vols. Detroit: Thomas-Gale, 2003.

———. "The Struggle of Religious Women for Eucharist." *Benedictines* 52 (1999): 12–25.

Obadia, Lionel. "Spirituality." In *The Wiley-Blackwell Encyclopedia of Social Theory,* edited by Bryan S. Turner and others. 5 vols. (2017). https://doi.org/10.1002/9781118430873.est0373.

L'Osservatore Romano. "Statutes Approved for the Association of Perpetual Eucharistic Adoration" (5 August 1991): 8.

Peacocke, Arthur. *Creation and the World of Science: The Re-Shaping of Belief.* Oxford: Oxford University Press, 2004 (1979).

Picucci, Egidio. "Le Quarantore nei documenti pontifici e nella pietà del Popolo di Dio." *L'Osservatore Romano,* edizione quotidiana (2–3 May 2005).

Pius XII, Pope. *Mediator Dei.* 20 November 1947. http://www.vatican.va/content/pius-xii/en/encyclicals/documents/hf_p-xii_enc_20111947_mediator-dei.html.

Pontifical Council for the Laity. *Directory: International Associations of the Faithful.* Rome: Libreria Editrice Vaticana, 2006.

Principe, Walter. "Towards Defining Spirituality." *Sciences Religieuses* 12, no. 2 (1983): 127–41.

Rahner, Karl. "An Earthly Mysticism." In *The Great Church Year: The Best of Karl Rahner's Homilies, Sermons, and Meditations,* edited by Albert Raffelt and Harvey Egan, 238. New York: Crossroad, 1994.

Ridley, Joan. *In the Presence: The Spirituality of Eucharistic Adoration.* Liguori, MO: Liguori, 2010.

Rituale Romanum (1614). Rome: Typographia Camerae Apostolicae, 1617.

Rosenzweig, Michael. *Win-Win Ecology: How the Earth's Species Can Survive in the Midst of Human Enterprise*. New York: Oxford University Press, 2003.

Rubin, Miri. *Corpus Christi: The Eucharist in Late Medieval Culture*. Cambridge: Cambridge University Press, 1991.

Ruddy, Christopher. "Pope and Abbot." *America* (22 May 2006). https://www.americamagazine.org/issue/573/article/pope-and-abbot.

Russell, James. *The Germanization of Early Medieval Christianity: A Sociohistorical Approach to Religious Transformation*. New York: Oxford University Press, 1994.

Schillebeeckx, Edward. *Christ, The Sacrament of the Encounter with God*. New York: Sheed and Ward, 1963.

Schneiders, Sandra. "Spirituality in the Academy." *Theological Studies* 50 (1989): 676–97.

Spadaro, Antonio. "A Big Heart Open to God: An Interview with Pope Francis." *America* (30 September 2013). https://www.america magazine.org/faith/2013/09/30/big-heart-open-god-interview-pope-francis.

Taft, Robert. "Is There Devotion to the Holy Eucharist in the Christian East?" *Worship* 80 (2006): 213–33.

Tagle, Luis Antonio. "L'adoration authentique." *Lumen Vitae* 64, no. 3 (2009): 291–98.

Thurston, Herbert. "The Early Cultus of the Blessed Sacrament." *Month* 109 (1907): 377–90.

———. "Forty Hours' Devotion" (6:151–53). In *The Catholic Encyclopedia*, edited by Charles Herbermann. 15 vols. New York: Robert Appleton, 1909.

Turksson, Peter. "Adoration as the Foundation of Social Justice." In *From Eucharistic Adoration to Evangelization*, edited by Alcuin Reid, 167–76. London: Burns and Oates, 2012.

van den Goorbergh, Edith. "Clare's Prayer as a Spiritual Journey." *Greyfriars Review* 10, no. 3 (1996): 283–92.

von Marienwerder, Johannes. *The Life of Dorothea von Montau: A Fourteenth-Century Recluse*. Translated by Ute Stargardt. Studies in Women and Religion. Vol. 39. Lewiston, NY: Edwin Mellen Press, 1997.

Walters, Barbara, Vincent Corrigan, and Peter Rickets. *The Feast of Corpus Christi*. University Park, PA: Pennsylvania State University Press, 2006.

Warners, David, Michael Ryskamp, and Randall Van Dragt. "Reconciliation Ecology: A New Paradigm for Advancing Creation Care." *Perspectives on Science and Faith* 66, no. 4 (December 2014): 221–35.

West, Fritz. *Scripture and Memory: The Ecumenical Hermeneutic of the Three-Year Lectionaries*. Collegeville, MN: Liturgical Press, 1997.

Whitehead, James D., and Evelyn Eaton Whitehead. *Method in Ministry: Theological Reflection and Christian Ministry*. Rev. ed. Kansas City: Sheed and Ward, 1995.

Wilken, Robert. *The Myth of Christian Beginnings*. Notre Dame: University of Notre Dame Press, 1971.

Zizioulas, John D. "Ecological Asceticism: A Cultural Revolution." *Sourozh* 67 (1997): 22–25.